MW00460073

HAVERIM

PAUL CLAYTON GIBBS

HOW TO STUDY ANYTHING WITH ANYONE

Part of the Ancient Trilogy

Haverim: How to Study Anything with Anyone
Copyright © 2017 by Paul Clayton Gibbs

Published by Harris House Publishing
harrishousepublishing.com
Colleyville, Texas
USA

Previously published as Haverim: The Four Lost Levels of Study (2013).

This title is available in other formats on amazon.com and paismovement.com/resources.

Cover creation by Andrew Sherrington; design by Paul Clayton Gibbs
Author's photo by Lena Gresser
Production team: Terry Tamashiro Harris | Rebecca Royal | Andrew Sherrington

All Scripture quotations, unless otherwise indicated, are taken from the Holy Bible, *New International Version®*, NIV®. Copyright ©1973, 1978, 1984, 2011 by Biblica, Inc.™ Used by permission of Zondervan. All rights reserved worldwide. www.zondervan.com. The "NIV" and "New International Version" are trademarks registered in the United States Patent and Trademark Office by Biblica, Inc.™

Scripture quotations marked NLT are taken from the Holy Bible, New Living Translation, copyright ©1996, 2004, 2007, 2013, 2015 by Tyndale House Foundation. Used by permission of Tyndale House Publishers, Inc., Carol Stream, Illinois 60188. All rights reserved.

Scripture quotations marked KJV are from The King James Version. The KJV is public domain in the United States.

Library of Congress Cataloging-in-Publication Data

Gibbs, Paul Clayton, 1964 -
     Haverim: How to Study Anything with Anyone / Paul Clayton Gibbs
         p.cm
     Includes biographical references
     ISBN 978-1-946369-21-5 (pbk.)
     1. Bible—Study and teaching. 2. Christianity and Culture. I. Title.
BS600.3.G53   2013
                         2013935797

All rights reserved. No portion of this book may be reproduced, stored in a retrieval system, or transmitted in any form or by any means—electronic, mechanical, photocopy, recording, or any other—except for brief quotation in printed reviews, without the prior permission of the publisher.

Printed in the United States of America.

This book is dedicated to

*Harry Letson for passing on your desire to study
and the courage to look at different angles*

*Henny Letson for the constant
encouragement every time I taught*

*Paul & Paula, John & Karen, Ian & Jan
for making it about Jesus and not religion*

#haverimdevotions

JOIN THE DISCUSSION
haverimdevotions.com

Contents

IMAGINE

From *push* to *pull.*

Why?

Dim

I once decided to read through the Bible in a year.

So, while working as a young manager in a department store, I spent every lunch hour, as well as the shorter morning and afternoon tea breaks, in a small room at the back of the building. While everyone else was in the canteen, I pored over my Bible and study aid, determined to reach my goal within 12 months. And, as an added bonus to my spiritual development, every Friday I fasted.

I grew in my knowledge of the chronological order of the Bible: its people, places, events, and teachings. And now, as I look over my life, I realize . . .

It was one of the most shortsighted things I ever did.

I spent an entire year, avoiding my co-workers in the cafeteria, to study about God's heart for my co-workers in the cafeteria.

God has put brains in our heads, conscience in our hearts, and His Spirit in our lives. So why did it take my colleagues challenging me about my lack of friendship to snap me out of it?

Was it because church culture had taught me to read the Bible without giving me an equal understanding of how to share it?

The Bible has a greater purpose than just simply developing individuals. It is intended to impact the world. While many great Bible studies provide for personal growth, it is my conviction that we need to find a better way to study in order to advance the Kingdom.

Recently I read a survey which stated that only 36% of Christian parents are likely to pass on their faith to their children, compared to 85% of Muslim parents who will.[1] We do not want to force our beliefs on our sons and daughters, but do we lack the understanding of how to teach the Word of God any other way?

As a result, are we producing pre-Reformation Christians in these post-modern times?

Before the Reformation, when the only organized and recognized church was the Catholic Church of Rome, Scripture was not available or allowed in any language other than Latin. The people of God had to rely completely on those few religious professionals who could pass on the Bible's message. They could not unravel it for themselves. No one could question an interpretation because few people other than priests could read it. For the most part in some of today's churches, the Bible may as well be written only in Latin once again.

USE

Few study it.

Even fewer pass it on.

Some of us rely on interpretation from the leaders we admire. In fact, many of us are more likely to know the words of Max, Bill, Rick, and Francis than we are to know the words of Matthew, Mark, Luke, and John.[2] We may not live in the *dark* ages anymore, but when it comes to understanding the Word of God, we live in the days of willing ignorance, the era of acceptable limitations.

We live in the '*dim* ages.'

Reformation

For years, I searched for a way to help people engage with Scripture. A way for us to not only study the Bible ourselves, but to help our colleagues at work, our fellow students, and the people in our communities discover it as well.

 A way to help *anybody* study *anything* with *anyone*.

In the process, I have come to realize that we need a new kind of Reformation—not so much in our theology but our methodology. A way to understand Scripture that is easily transferable and does not require a Ph.D. in order to teach it to others. My aim has been to rediscover what Jesus had in mind when His Spirit prompted the writer of Hebrews to note that:

> In fact, though by this time you ought to be teachers, you need some-
> one to teach you the elementary truths of God's word all over again.
> You need milk, not solid food! [3]

As the Church, we have reformed our worship, leading to greater numbers of people attending our contemporary services and connecting more deeply with God emotionally. Yet, how many congregations have put that same amount of effort into reforming our Bible studies? And what will be the eventual consequences of a generation led by their world of feelings rather than the Word of God?

Over the last 25 years as the leader of Pais, an organization that has recruited thousands of Christians and placed them on the mission field, I have noticed that the Biblical literacy of our new applicants seems to be lower than it once was. More significantly, their understanding of Biblical authority has also decreased. As a larger number of millennials join us, fewer and fewer are coming to us from churches that have equipped them with a passion or process to discover the Word of God.

They love to worship but they do not know how to study.

Many years ago, I was training a youth pastor in how to teach Scripture. A few minutes into our time together, he turned to me and said, "I don't know why we need to learn this; young people need to know we love them before they will want listen to us!"

"That's true," I replied. "The problem is that when they finally want to listen to you . . . you will have nothing to say."

His teaching was shallow, consisting of a stream of Christian clichés he had heard in church.

And so, I began asking my question:

> How do I equip people who have the desire to change their world with the ability to actually do it?

Epic

Then one day, my worlds collided: the community of millennials I lead and that of the ancient rabbis I studied.

I had launched into what I originally considered two completely separate research projects. In the first, I was exploring the values of postmodernity and in the second, the rabbinic teaching methods of the Second Temple period. Suddenly these two separate studies came into focus in the same way you look through a pair of binoculars, turning the diopter settings until the two lenses sync and the view becomes crystal clear. Paradoxically, I began finding the answer to my questions about training *postmodern* young adults in the *ancient* methods of Jesus and His contemporaries.

It turned out that Jesus had all the right answers!

 Actually, it turned out that He had all the right *questions*.

I had discovered that most books on postmodernity were not really about postmodernity at all, but were just commentaries on the modern world and how it was changing. In one book, however, author Leonard Sweet points out that even though we don't really know what this new age will fully look like, we can recognize some of its emerging values,[4] values that I believe are fulfilled in the Bible study process I will share with you in this book.

The author uses the acronym of E.P.I.C. to explain them. I have made some slight alterations and included my own brief interpretation to help us see the opportunities.

Experiential: In the modern world, instructions were given to be *executed*; in this emerging world, invitations are offered to be *experienced*.

Participatory: In the modern world, opportunities were presented to be *performed*; in this emerging world, people are encouraged to *participate*.

Imaginative: In the modern world, images were used to *present answers*; in this emerging world, images are required to *provoke questions*.

Connected: In the modern world, *consumption* drove individualism; in this emerging world, *connectivity* recreates consumerism.

As you ponder these simple values, perhaps you can relate to them. I know I can. I also see how Jesus's methods of grasping truth and passing it on mesh so very well with them.

I feel hope.

I am encouraged.

I found a way forward.

What?

Pull

My friend Matt works at an influential advertising agency.

He often helps me think through our use of social media to promote the mission of the Pais Movement. We share resources; I have taught at his workplace as a consultant, and he has spoken at various Pais conferences. According to Matt, the advertising industry has had to respond to a fundamental shift within society in the last decade. In the past, agencies like his determined what the customer heard and saw. More recently, however, through the internet and other interactive technologies, the customers decide for themselves what they see.

Information, learning, and understanding face a new methodology:

> From *push* to *pull*.

In the past, advertisements were *pushed* onto potential customers, but now those same people only *pull* the information they are interested in. Have you noticed that the way you want to learn is changing? I see it in my two sons. According to *The New York Times*, they are the first generation to actually watch *less* television than their elders.[5] Instead of being presented with a pre-determined menu of limited options, they hit the internet like ravenous wolves, seeking out the things that interest them. They have become expert researchers.

This bodes well for the Kingdom if we can facilitate the discovery of truth in God's Word.

Many believe that something has changed regarding how we are now shaped to receive information. For instance, recent generations are rejecting much of the modern era's packaging of simplistic cause-and-effect solutions. Easy answers, put in a simple, relevant way, are not in vogue as they once were. However, I wonder, has that really changed or was the Bible always best grasped in a different way? Is it true that we find the Bible difficult to understand, *or* is it truer to say that our difficulty stems from the way it is taught?

Does the Bible have a middle-management problem?

I think it does.

We need, therefore, to go beyond *curriculum* to *culture.*

A culture where the average Christian knows how to study the Bible for themselves and how to help others discover it also. I long for a time when the Bible is once again used as the evangelistic tool that it was meant to be:

> *Philip ran over and heard the man reading from the prophet Isaiah. Philip asked, "Do you understand what you are reading?" The man replied, "How can I, unless someone instructs me?" And he urged Philip to come up into the carriage and sit with him.*[6]

If we truly believe that God will change our world and use us to do it, then now is the time to build our large, contemporary, relevant churches with *His* understanding of Bible study in mind.

The inventor Sir James Dyson said that reinvention requires a passionate anger about something that doesn't work.[7] And something isn't working, is it?

By that, I mean the purely invitational approach that first brings in a crowd through a great presentation, and then follows up with optional Bible studies for those wanting to fill in blanks on a worksheet. *That* idea is compromised, incomplete, and shortsighted. *Oh snap!*

It can grow *congregations*, but does it advance His *Kingdom*?

In many churches, only core members attend Bible studies, and they rarely experience a method of study that can be easily reproduced in other settings or for other passages and topics.

A modern Bible class teaches people *what* to study, not *how* to study.

I am committed to getting people on the same page and drawing them to absolute truth. The problem with most curriculums, however, is that they ultimately teach us to search for answers, and by answers I mean the *one* answer of the *one* presenter. Once we know that one answer, we quickly become bored. The Word of God becomes cliché: something profound, but weakened by constant repetition of the same one-dimensional explanations.

This creates two initial problems.

1 First, it loses its vitality and loses its surprise.

Since introducing Haverim, many Christians, particularly those who have attended church for decades, have expressed a fresh new interest in Scripture. They often admit that they thought they had pretty much heard everything before . . . every story, every letter, every perspective. They had grown a little weary with the Bible. But Haverim changed that because it opens up an infinite treasure chest of new things to learn and do.

2 A second problem is that our modern method of study does not equip us to share that truth with others. It only offers our church members programs to which they can bring people. We put on a particular course or series and hope that it may interest those we wish to invite. But what if they have different questions?

What if we are *pushing* what they are not looking to *pull* from us?

We live in a new world, with new opportunities and the need for a new transferable way to share the Gospel.

15

I believe Haverim fulfills this challenge in a fresh and exciting way.

As I write this chapter, I am sitting at a table in my local coffee shop. Nearby sits an older gentleman who is smartly dressed and a touch debonair. He has just tucked a paper napkin into his collar as he tries to avoid dripping mayonnaise while negotiating a turkey and cheese sandwich. I am wondering how I can start a conversation with him.

If I do manage to chat with him and he shows an interest in discovering faith in Jesus, I know that I now have a new way of sharing it with him—one that approaches the Bible from whatever angle *he* needs to approach it, one that will present questions not just answers, and one that will guide him through a multi-faceted journey until he can discover for himself the truth of Jesus.

I am also sitting here wondering how other followers of Jesus would feel in my position right now. Would they even want to start that conversation, or would they avoid it because they have no idea how to unpack the Scriptures with a neighbor?

Is the spirit willing but the training weak?

I think it may be.

Haverim

Haverim has its roots in a rabbinical process from the Second Temple period.[8]

It is part of a trilogy of books that offers a rediscovery of ancient methods. The books can be read in any order. The second book, *Talmidim*, shows us how to disciple anyone in anything and the third, *Shalom*, teaches us how to reach anyone, anywhere. There are crossovers throughout the books and I would encourage you to read all three for a comprehensive and alternative way to approach the following pillars of our faith: mission, discipleship, and study.

Whereas *Talmidim* teaches us how to reproduce the *practices* of Christianity and *Shalom* how to spread the *message* of Christianity, this book is used to help us explore and pass on the *beliefs* of Christianity.

Haver means 'friends,' and in Biblical times, the word *haverim* specified 'friends who studied together.'

All over the world—in Europe, Africa, Asia, North America, Australia, and South America—through Pais and those we are connecting with, young and old are exploring this new, yet ancient, method on a daily basis as part of a Haverim group.

Later in the *infrastructure* section of this book, I will share some ideas of how Haverims can be organized. I will also unpack ideas for using it with non-Christians and different age groups. Plus, I will take you through an example of a Haverim study from beginning to end.

Before that, however, I want to concentrate on a key part of the Haverim process: the *way* in which we study together. We call it Haverim Devotions™ and it has four levels or ancient practices that are used to study the Bible.[9] Each level varies from the other, often appealing to different personality types and incorporating the different learning styles, but always aiming to uncover something more about God's purpose. People are different and Haverim Devotions takes advantage of that. One of the levels is especially attractive to those who love *research*, one for those who enjoy *riddles*, one for those who find pleasure in deepening *relationships*, and one for those who love *reflecting*.

I have given an English name to each of these Hebraic practices:

The *intended* meaning (*p'shat*)

The *implied* meaning (*r'mez*)

The *interpreted* meaning (*d'rash*)

The *inspired* meaning (*s'od*)

Every level gives a fresh perspective, and each new perspective produces fresh results.

In this book, I will explain *why* each level of Haverim Devotions is especially beneficial, *what* to do, and *how* to do it. I will include the *specific* questions to ask and the *action points* that make the levels so dynamic.

The method can be used for individual study, but that is not its main purpose. Neither is it limited to providing another Bible study program in a church. Instead, my intention is to spark a culture where the saints are equipped to teach the Word of God in their communities. The Church once again becomes a training center. Not the place to simply come and learn, but the place to come and learn how to go and teach.

Ideally, once members of a congregation are trained, they will start Haverim groups or use the method to share their insights with their colleagues, families, and neighbors. They will gather people who seek to gain a deeper understanding of God . . . whether they are followers of Jesus or only seekers of Him. Therefore, much of this book deals with how individuals can study with their friends, either in groups they set up themselves or as part of a wider organization.

Haverim Devotions can also be used by leaders to pass on Bible teaching that they specifically want to teach. This can take place during the third level. I will explain how that is accomplished in the chapters that unpack the *interpreted* meaning.

A Haverim is inclusive.

It is open to everyone who is leaning forward.

Haverims throughout the world are adopting Jesus's philosophy of teaching those who want to be taught. So this way of studying is open to an agnostic, an atheist, a Muslim, a Hindu, a non-practicing or disconnected Christian, etc. The only requisite is that it does require a person to be leaning forward—a person who is searching for more.

If you are a follower of Jesus, can I encourage you to practice studying the Scripture in this way so that it becomes second nature to you? As it does, you will be able to spot where people are on their journey and you will be equipped to assist them.

Haverim Devotions is not a list of steps to execute, but an invitation to come and experience. It is not a presentation tool, but a participation tool. It does not simply provide the right answers, but it provokes the right questions. All of this is because Haverim is not an opportunity to just consume knowledge, but to connect with others in order to share it.

In doing so, Haverim will take us beyond head knowledge and help transform hearts.

How?

Pardes

The pursuit of God's heart started a long time ago in a world distant, yet not so distinct, from ours.

During the middle ages, rabbis looked back on the time of Jesus and noticed various methods of both understanding and teaching the Word of God that were used in the Second Temple period.

Some named this methodology *PaRDeS*.[10]

Pardes is a word with Persian origins and means 'orchard,' 'park,' or more specifically, a 'garden of knowledge.'

Later hijacked by mystics and Gnostics, some of its many benefits have been lost to us. In fact, although understanding *pardes* has helped shed light on the teaching of Jesus, I have not found a single Christian book written solely on the subject.

Did we throw out the baby with the bath water? Or, is it that we simply have thought so little of the importance of Jesus's culture that we never ran the bath in the first place?

Although the term *pardes* was unlikely to have existed in the time of Jesus, the word itself hints at His ancient and dynamic form of teaching. It reminds us that much of a rabbi's ministry occurred within the community, perhaps under a tree or atop a grassy hill, with eager students and disciples experiencing not just the words, but participating in the actions of their role model.

PaRDeS is where we derive the word 'paradise' from, and it is an acronym of four parts:

> *P'shat*
> *R'mez*
> *D'rash*
> *S'od*

To develop Haverim Devotions, I took these ancient ideas, untangling and reworking them in order to transfer them into the world in which we live today. They resulted in what I believe are straightforward steps that help unravel the Word of God. I have found them to be phenomenal for engaging those who want to *experience, participate, imagine,* and *connect* in order to search for the heart of God. They also help those simply searching for a God to know.

Each level of Haverim Devotions consists of two types of questions or instructions, plus one *action point*. I have included practical applications and will share creative ideas to implement each of the levels.

I am presenting them not to tickle academic thinking, but to equip the saints for works of service.

I have reshaped, rethought, reformatted, and retold them.

What I have not done is reengineer their dynamics.

Fable

Before we begin to unpack this way of studying, it is important that we understand what it is for and what it is not for.

Haverim Devotions offers the opportunity to search for not only the heart of God, but for the mind of Christ. That journey, however, must be undertaken for all the right reasons.

A fable in Jewish folklore about the four levels of *pardes* goes:

> Four men entered paradise. One looked and died; one looked and
> went mad; one destroyed the plants; and one entered in peace and
> departed in peace.[11]

This is interpreted to mean that four men searched for the 'secret knowl-edge' of God. The first died a spiritual death and lost what he once had. The second went mad. The third committed heresy. Only the fourth left in peace.

How you enter the Word of God will often determine how you leave it. This Jewish folklore warns us of the age-old dangers of searching for God's secret wisdom.

It is not for *status*.

We should not seek understanding in order to prove ourselves better than others. One of the dangers in getting perhaps too engrossed in Judaism and its rituals is that we may fall afoul of the religious pride that seems to accompany it. Jesus taught us that true wisdom is seen in those who are truly humble.

It is not for *salvation*.

The secrets of the mystical religions of Jesus's day were believed to be nec-essary for redemption. These mystery religions were exclusive. Only certain people could ever know their secrets. They were esoteric in nature. Jesus stressed that salvation comes through Him and that *anyone* who seeks will find.

So, if it is not for status and it is not for salvation, what *is* it for?

It is for *establishing*.

Establishing on earth the Kingdom of Heaven.

Establishing the Kingdom within your heart to such an extent that it over-flows into your world.

Haverim asks a question:

> Do you want to see what Jesus sees, feel what the Father feels, and join in what His Spirit is doing?

INTENDED

P'shat | Context | Point

Why?

Surface

Imagine that when the Word of God hits your heart it could go deeper than the surface.

The Parable of the Soils in Matthew 13 should really be titled 'The Parable of the Hearers.'[12] Describing the different conditions onto which seed falls, it is Jesus's version of a popular analogy of His time that intended to point out the four ways people receive and respond to truth.[13]

In this particular case, the truth is the message of the Kingdom of God.

> *". . . Some fell along the path, and the birds came and ate it up."*[14]

The path represents those who don't really understand their place in the Kingdom, and so life gobbles up the message before it can even find a place to root. The little they misunderstood is snatched away.

Ever felt that your understanding of God's Word was superficial?

Ever felt that you've followed God for superficial reasons?

Maybe there is a connection.

To make Jesus's words fully relevant to *our* culture, it helps if we first understand *His*.

A true commitment to the *intended* meaning will protect us from the temptation to which we are all prone—the temptation to cut and paste Scripture in a way that will best promote our personal agenda. Perhaps most importantly, however, it provides a safety net for all the adventure, excitement, and freedom that comes from exploring the deeper, more creative levels.

As the rabbis put it:

> "No scripture ever loses its *p'shat*." [15]

In other words, this *intended* meaning stops us from coming up with crazy interpretations of Scripture when we engage in some of the more flamboyant, fun, and unique exercises that we will discover later on. It does this by making sure we never lose sight of the obvious point it is making.

Puzzle

God has planted hidden things. He has not hidden them *from* us but *for* us. He has hidden them for when we are ready to understand them.

He has hidden things in nature, and the more we discover about our universe, the more we see signs and metaphors of God's plan and wisdom, His nature and super-nature.

He has hidden things in humankind; the ways our bodies work are biological object lessons. The more we discover about the body, the more we learn about His plan for the body of Christ.

For this reason, the point of a passage is best understood by discovering its context.

Consider this puzzle:

> I cdnuolt blveiee taht I cluod aulaclty uesdnatnrd waht I was raednig. The aamizng pweor of the hmuan mind! Aoccdrnig to rscheearch at Cmabrigde Uinervtisy, it deosn't mttaer in waht oredr the ltteers in a wrod are, the olny iprmoatnt tihng is taht the frist and lsat ltteer are in the rghit pclae. The rset can be a tatol mses and you can sitll raed it wouthit a porbelm.

It is interesting to me that this ability was wired into our brains long before English was invented. It works for most western languages but not for others such as Hebrew.

What is the implication here?

Well, please read these two sentences:

> A vheclie epxledod at a plocie cehckipont naer the UN haduqertares in Bagahdd on Mnoday kilinlg the bmober and an Irqai polcie offceir.

And then read this:

> The cghunaninm ctroonls teh froe and aft psiioton of dfart in the gnoea and wkors wtih the tlveerar, measheint, oauhutl and vnag to ozimptie sial sphae.

The same rules apply, but for most people the second sentence is much harder to read.

Why? Because we do not understand its *context*. It involves sailing terms and practices that most of us are unfamiliar with; therefore, we find it harder to make sense of the message.

The first level of Haverim Devotions will teach us how to find the *context* required to comprehend God's *point* . . . not because we cannot see His point, but because we may be so engulfed by our culture and unaware of the culture in which it was written that we cannot see it clearly.

The rabbis taught in gardens. Sometimes they sat down to teach in synagogues or the portico of the temple, but more often they taught in vineyards, orchards, and parks. In doing so, they were able to help their disciples taste their *Torah*.[16] They could see the starkness of a withered fig tree; they could enjoy the beauty of a field of lilies. They could touch the good soil that crumbled in their fingers or feel the sun-scorched path beneath their feet. They could scratch their ankles on the wild thorns or twist them while walking on a rocky outcrop.

They were not just listening to their rabbi's teaching; they were *absorbing* it.

When we miss His *context*, we can miss His *point*.

Just like the second puzzle, we may struggle to put the pieces together.

What?

Context

The first level of Haverim Devotions looks for the *intended* meaning.

The *intended* meaning is the obvious, straightforward message of a passage.

The Hebrew word for this level is *p'shat* and means 'simple.'

The method of the *intended* meaning is to seek *context* in order to find the *point*.

The Bible comes to light when you can start to *feel* the setting in which it was happening. So we do this by engaging in a discovery of its history, culture, and timeline. Often we can miss the main point of what Jesus was saying because we no longer understand *how* He was saying it, *when* He was saying it, or even *why* He was saying it. At times, this can lead to misunderstanding and confusion, especially giving rise to the idea that the Bible contradicts itself.

Later we will look at how we can discover context without having to be a historian, Bible scholar, or archaeologist, but first, let me give you examples of the insights and benefits I have discovered at this level.

In one culture-shaping bit of history, the Bible records when Nicodemus, a member of the Sanhedrin, approached Jesus. In this conversation, Jesus employed the famous 'born again' phrase. Many think that Jesus coined the idiom 'born again' and that the phrase itself had never before been heard by Nicodemus.

But He did not and it had been.

A study of context teaches us that the maxim 'born again' and its variations already existed in Jesus's day. In fact, six uses of it were well known.[17] You were born again when:

1. You got married.

2. You converted and were baptized into Judaism.

3. You became a son of the commandments.

4. You were ordained as a rabbi.

5. You became leader of a rabbinical school.

6. You were crowned King of Israel.

All of these were major life changes and none were likely to happen to Nicodemus due to his age. Imagine his surprise. What did Jesus mean? What options were left? Was he to re-enter his mother's womb?

What exactly was Jesus emphasizing? What was His message? Well, what did He say next?

> "Very truly I tell you, no one can enter the Kingdom of God unless they are born of water and the Spirit."[18]

And the *Spirit*.

The six uses of 'born again' were rituals of some sort.

Consummation

Ordination

Coronation

But Jesus was emphasizing that a ceremony could not save you. He was getting at something else, something to do with the Spirit. I believe in justification by faith, but this fresh understanding made me question if I had led people to believe that just a moment of faith is required. Following Jesus is not about a moment of faith but a lifestyle of faith . . . a commitment not simply to rules and regulations but to a relationship.

Could I have made the mistake of missing His context and inadvertently encouraged people to think they are born again by simply raising their hands or saying a prayer? How should this better understanding of Jesus's message affect my methods?

It is the Spirit, not a ritual, which reproduces Jesus in our lifestyle. *And the Spirit'* is the key to a life of faith.

When Jesus used the phrase with Nicodemus, He was presenting a commitment to follow the Spirit of God, not simply the traditions of men. Jesus was not making things easy for Nicodemus; He was outlining to Israel's teacher what would come after a decision to follow Him. That has been helpful to me as I train missionaries around the world. I advise them to share the Gospel in a way that does not simply end with a prayer so their sins will be forgiven but to let people know up front exactly what they are getting into if they receive Christ as their Savior.

In summary, I teach them: "Easy in, easy out."

Without a commitment to follow the Holy Spirit's prompting in our lives, we accept an invitation to the wrong party. Jesus's context requires me to ask the question, "Am I in danger of simply adding number seven to the list of rituals?"

   7. You put your hand up in the air after an altar call.

In this case at least, seven is not a lucky number.

Delay

Sometimes Jesus confuses me.

Consider, for instance, the account of Lazarus's death recorded in John 11.

When Jesus is told that His friend is seriously sick, He seems at first hard-hearted, apathetic, or at best, distracted. Rather than rushing to Lazarus's aid, Jesus delays His trip for a couple of days, arriving after the man has died and been entombed.

Why delay? Why create more anxiety than needed? Why allow His friends to feel pain? Why appear to encourage doubt?

Specifically, the Bible tells us Lazarus had been entombed for four days.[19] This is important.

The Bible does not contain any FYIs.

If it is specific, it is significant!

The Pharisees taught, and many Jews believed, that the spirit hovered over a dead body for three days. It was believed that a person could be 'resuscitated' within that time. Even today there are often medical reports of people 'dying' for minutes on a surgeon's table but then coming back to life. The Jews, therefore, even had a custom called *Shiv'ah*, meaning 'seven.' The mourners would mourn very heavily for the first three days, then heavily for the next four, and then lightly for the rest of the month. These first three days were intensely sorrowful but laced with hope.[20]

Jesus had raised people from the dead soon after their death and so had other Biblical heroes, but in Jewish history, no one had been raised from the dead after four days.[21] After researching various sources for a better understanding of the context, I discovered that the Jews believed that only the Messiah could do this!

Jesus delayed in order to heal after the fourth day. He did it to create understanding of *who* He was, not simply *what* He could do. I realized through the *intended* level that sometimes Jesus delays His answer to my prayers because what is more important than an answer is *understanding* the answer.

Jesus delayed in order that people might put their hope in Him . . . not in what He could do.

Kosher

Sometimes we miss the point because we didn't even know there was a point to be made.

Soon after the birth of the Church, something very unexpected happened. The Gentiles were born again and filled with the Spirit, and so the disciples, realizing that God had a plan for these new 'Christians,' reported their findings to the Council of Jerusalem.

Shortly afterwards, some of the Pharisees demanded that these new converts be circumcised and be required to obey the Law of Moses. The Council, therefore, had a problem. What advice should they give them? What instructions? They spent some time discussing and seeking discernment from the Holy Spirit, and then they simply declared:

> It seemed good to the Holy Spirit and to us not to burden you with anything beyond the following requirements: You are to abstain from food sacrificed to idols, from blood, from the meat of strangled animals and from sexual immorality. You will do well to avoid these things.[22]

The best way to study the Word of God is to be driven by questions. The biggest and most important question is, "What is His Word trying to teach us about the heart of God?" It is this question added to a study of the context that helps us discover something very important to God that we might otherwise have missed.

Examining the *intended* meaning of this passage encouraged me to ask the following questions:

Were these the only commandments that these Gentiles needed to observe?

Why was such importance placed on the food laws?

Why not emphasize many of the other Laws of Moses . . . like do not murder?

When I ask most Christians what they think the Jews believed about the Gentiles and if they could be saved, the general response is that they had not really thought about it before. Some thought that the Jews believed the Gentiles could not be saved; others suggested that the Gentiles would have to convert to Judaism. Both of these answers make sense when you skim the surface of the Bible without even delving into the first level of context.

But here is what I discovered at the first level of Haverim . . .

For a very long time, well before this story in Acts, the Jews believed that the Gentiles could be part of *Olam Haba*, 'the world to come,' a Jewish euphemism for what we might call Heaven. In Jesus's day, such Gentiles were known as 'God-fearers,' and they were given a place in the temple called the Court of the Gentiles. The God-fearers would commit to the Noahide Laws.[23] These laws, listed by the *Tosefta* and the *Talmud*, originated in Genesis 9.

Prohibition of idolatry

Prohibition of murder

Prohibition of theft

Prohibition of sexual immorality

Prohibition of blasphemy

Prohibition of eating flesh taken from an animal while it is still alive

Establishment of courts of law

So when James stood up at the Council of Jerusalem, it was already understood that these new converts would need to live by the Noahide Laws such as do not murder. That's my first question answered.

But why emphasize the particular food restrictions that added to them? After all, had Jesus not previously declared certain foods clean?

This question leads us to understand something very important about God's heart for His people. This additional emphasis prompted by the Spirit was given so that the Gentiles could sit down to a meal and break bread with their Jewish brothers who would otherwise be restricted socially because of the Law of Moses.

The *intended* level helps me understand that even though the Gentiles did not have to obey the food restrictions, they did it to fulfill the spirit of the law. God, they realized, saw their commitment to Him through their commitment to His people. In the same way, although I may have freedom in Christ to do my own thing, I will sometimes want to restrict that freedom in order to be a better member of the family of God.

P'shat means 'simple.'

The simple meaning of a passage is just the beginning.

How?

Intended

So how exactly do we study at this level and lead others through it?

We ask questions.

Some questions are *specific* and some are *generic*.

The *specific* question varies and is determined by the overall thought into which the Haverim wants to look. Usually there is only one *specific* question. It will guide the group to gain insight on something that may be difficult to understand about the passage.

The *specific* question may be prompted by the following:

> What seems odd that might be better understood with an increased knowledge of its context?

The *generic* questions are:

> Who wrote it?
> Why did they write it?
> Where were they when they wrote it?
> How is it affected by the manners and customs of the day?
> What can archaeology teach us about this passage?
> What does history teach us about the subject?
> What happened to the main character(s) before or after the incident?

When explored in a Haverim, we can ask these questions as one large group or split into smaller groups with each group working on different questions. Importantly, I rarely organize people to research by themselves. Why? So that newbies will not feel exposed, and so that one person can train another younger, less experienced, or less mature member how to study.

Each level also has an *action point*.

For the *intended* level, the *action point* is:

> Share what the context taught you about the main point of the passage.

After an allotted amount of research time, we allow time for each group to share their findings with the rest of the Haverim. Then, using the *action point*, we encourage everyone to summarize the intended meaning of the passage.

Tools

We equip our groups with a variety of tools to search out their answers.

Obviously, if you are leading a group, you may want to provide these resources initially with the hope that your friends will learn how to use them and begin to resource themselves.

Typically, general resource books or online tools should be available each time the group meets. On occasion, as mentioned later in the Infrastructure section of the book, you may want to provide a specific resource to ensure your Haverim discovers specific information.

Even as I am writing this, I know that my recommendations are quickly becoming outdated because many people in the Haverim on my street bring commentaries that are online and read them on their smartphones or tablets. Everything I list below can now be carried with you if you are fortunate enough to own one of these devices. Not only is it more practical to carry these books digitally, it is far less intimidating for those who do not own the books or are unfamiliar with them.

The following recommendations are generic. Depending on whether or not you are pioneering a Haverim group, taking part in one, or simply attempting to use the four levels of Haverim Devotions in your own personal study, these seven tools are ideal for discovering the *intended* meaning of a passage. They are certainly not the only ones, and I would encourage you not to limit the allowed resources in any way.

Commentary

A commentary is an interpretation of a passage. It may be based on a particular book or the entire Bible. A commentary may contain studies of words, phrases, history, parables, etc. In addition to the author's interpretation, it also brings contextual information to the passage.

There are roughly two types of commentaries. The first is a commentary within a Bible. In the past, I have used the *NIV Study Bible* and the *NLT Life Application Study Bible*, which both contain commentary on the Bible passages as you read them. These two study Bibles come from different perspectives. The first gives more factual information and the second offers observations on how you might apply a passage to yourself. Presently, I use the *NIV Archaeological Study Bible*, which comments on the history and culture of the passages.

The other type of commentary is a stand-alone one. These can come as individual books or as a series. To be honest, commentaries are like a piece of string; they can go on forever. My advice is that when you are gathering as a Haverim, depending on the situation, you may not wish to bring too many books; the first type of commentary (one contained within the Bible) plus online commentaries on your phone may be the best way forward.[24]

Encyclopedia

One particular type of handbook that I have found ideal for understanding context is a Biblical encyclopedia.[25] Some are specific to historical facts and archaeology. For the visually driven like myself, these books are extremely useful. They can usually be browsed by timeline and/or topic. Sometimes the information they throw out is a little pointless but adds color. Did you know, for instance, that popcorn was a staple diet for many people in Biblical days? Other information, however, vastly improves my understanding of a story, place, or person, and affects how I see even the simplest passage of Scripture.

Concordance

A concordance allows me to find a particular word or phrase, and then it lists the many passages of Scripture in which that word is also found. Again, this simple tool gives me the benefit of understanding. So let's say God uses a peculiar phrase to describe someone. A concordance can show me other instances where the phrase is used in the Bible. These other instances lead me to a fuller realization and appreciation of what He meant.

As with commentaries, you can find concordances within your Bible or as standalone books. In the past, I have used *Gruden's Complete Concordance to the Old and New Testaments*, but today I often use biblegateway.com as it provides not only an instant comprehensive list, but gives me the option to find the word in other translations.

Topical

A topical Bible or book brings out cultural and historical background about specific topics. Like encyclopedias, these books are useful for understanding parables, details about certain jobs, techniques, manners, or customs, and so much more. They come in all shapes and sizes. Some cover the entire Bible and others target specific topics. One of these books gave me a completely different perspective on how Jesus used parables; it helped me understand that in some cases He was not simply creating a new story but reshaping an existing one in order to emphasize what was truly important to the Father.[26]

Unlike some other resources, specific topical books are only brought to the Haverim when specific passages are being examined. So if we were studying Psalm 23 with a theme of shepherding, we would bring topical books that cover that kind of career.

Translations

Each translation of the Bible has a particular emphasis, and different insights can be gained by the different wording. Unlike most church services, which encourage people to quite literally be on the same page by reading the same version, in a Haverim group it is very useful for different people to bring different versions. This not only benefits us in the *intended* level but the *interpreted* level as well.

Certain Bibles make it easy to compare different translations by placing them together. These are called Parallel Bibles. Again, the invention of online Bibles and apps means that with the flick of a thumb you can switch translations and compare them.

Dictionary

Occasionally, a dictionary of difficult words or doctrines can be useful. Certain passages benefit greatly from this type of book if you are trying to understand peculiar or unfamiliar phrases in their context, particularly in the epistles.

If you remember, the *intended* level is our safety net. These books help ensure that we do not create a false theological perspective from an isolated comment or instruction because we are unfamiliar with the framework in which it is set.

Digital

As I have said, there are many digital versions of all the above, most of which are free on the internet or as apps. In addition, online resources encompass many, if not all of them. A good Haverim leader will keep seeking these out and passing them on to the group.

Here are just a few digital resources that people have posted on the Haverim Devotions Facebook group:

> biblegateway.com
>
> blueletterbible.org

thattheworldmayknow.com

thebibleproject.com

globible.com

chabad.org

biblestudytools.com

The other benefit of using digital resources is that the Haverim will be encouraged to share their findings on social media. There is a social media wall where you can use the hashtag #haverimdevotions so that your post, plus everyone else's, will appear on the wall.[27]

Not everyone will enjoy this *intended* level as much as they will enjoy the others, but it is without a doubt the one that gives us our Biblical foundation. It is like setting up a base camp at the foot of a mountain; it provides everything we need to go further and everything we require for our journey to stay on track.

Summary

So let me summarize a suggested process for the *intended* level.

At this level, the group utilizes a variety of books, websites, and other study resources to examine the context of the passage in order to discover its intended point. Organize the Haverim into groups of twos and threes. Discuss the *specific* question and assign the *generic* questions to each group, ignoring those not applicable to the passage. After an allotted time for research, ask each group to share its discoveries. Finally, use the *action point* to encourage each person to summarize the main point.

Specific Question:

> What seems odd that might be better understood with an increased knowledge of its context?

Generic Questions:

> Who wrote it?

Why did they write it?

Where were they when they wrote it?

How is it affected by the manners and customs of the day?

What can archaeology teach us about this passage?

What does history teach us about the subject?

What happened to the main character(s) before or after the incident?

Action Point:

Share what the context taught you about the main point of the passage.

IMPLIED

R'mez | Connections | Principle

Why?

Shallow

Imagine the possibility of discovering principles buried in God's Word.

> *"Some fell on rocky places, where it did not have much soil. It sprang up quickly, because the soil was shallow. But when the sun came up, the plants were scorched, and they withered because they had no root."*[28]

The rocky area in the Parable of the Soils refers to those who receive the message of the Kingdom with joy. They are pleased to hear about God's plan because it speaks to them of a better life. So, when persecution comes and when what they get is less than what they hoped for, it is easily uprooted. The joy they had is taken away.

Ever felt that your understanding of God's Word was shallow?

Ever felt that its effect on you should be even deeper?

Maybe there is a connection.

A story is told of the Prince of Granada who was locked away in prison for many years. Granted one request, he asked to be given a Bible and spent the entire time of incarceration alone with this one book. When he died, it was noted that the walls of his cell were filled with Bible trivia:

Psalm 118:8 is the middle verse of the Bible.

Ezra 7:21 contains all the letters of the alphabet except the letter J.

Esther 8:9 is the longest verse in the Bible.

No word or name with more than six syllables is found in Scripture.

It was said of the prince that he knew a book that never *changed* him.

His captors saw no sign in his behavior that its words had taken root, because studying the Bible without understanding its principles is full of lessons that are never truly learned.

Why? Because we cannot see the *connections*.

I recently heard the word 'genius' described as 'the ability to see patterns between isolated facts,' and this is surely the key to spiritual wisdom. It is this kind of wisdom that Jesus passed on to His disciples. He gave *patterns* and *principles* to those eager enough to find them. He filtered out those who were looking for easy answers in order to manipulate God, while the seekers of the Kingdom were equipped, not simply to know what to do in a *specific* situation, but with the understanding of how to determine God's will for *any* situation.

The second level of Haverim Devotions will empower us with that kind of wisdom. It will help us find the *connections* required to comprehend God's *principles*.

When I teach the second level of Haverim, I show a selection of artwork. I present three paintings from one artist, then three from another, and finally three paintings from a third. Then I present a final painting from one of the three. No matter how little my audience knows about art, and even though they have never seen this particular painting before, they instantly know who the artist is. They know because they have seen a pattern emerge. And this pattern, this way of painting, this recognition of style, allows them to easily spot the hand of the artist.

So it is with the Word of God.

The Bible becomes much more than spiritual graffiti.

What?

Connection

The second level of Haverim Devotions searches for the *implied* meaning.

The *implied* meaning is discovered through clues hidden in the passage.

The Hebrew word for this second level is *r'mez* and means 'hint.'

The method of the *implied* meaning is to seek *connections* that lead to a *principle*.

R'mez is where Scripture interprets Scripture. The Bible comes to our aid when it equips us with patterns of why what happened happened. If we miss its riddles, we miss the deeper values that God wants to teach us. This is where we have to make a decision:

Do we only want to learn *what* to think or are we eager to understand *how* to think?

If we miss His *connections*, we miss His *principles*. Not because we do not know they are there, but because we do not know how to find them. So at this level, we intentionally look for a principle to be discovered or a pattern to be noticed.

To first help us understand *r'mez*, here are some principles the *implied* level taught me.

Sticks

On the cross, Jesus utters these mortal words:

"My God, My God, why have you forsaken me?"[29]

So many questions.

For many years, I struggled with this. Had God forsaken Jesus? Why did He believe that God had forsaken Him? What on earth was going on?

I understand the usual answers—that the sin of the world was put on Jesus and God turned away from Him. This answer, however, just leads me to more questions.

At what point does sin get so bad that God will turn His face from us? Is there a place where we cross over a line and God forsakes us? Why did Jesus clearly believe that He would rise again and yet now declare that God had given up on Him? Was Jesus confused?

And most importantly, the question that nobody ever answers is this . . .

Why did Jesus say, *"Why?"*

If the Father had forsaken Him and He knew it was going to happen, wouldn't He simply have cried:

"My God, My God, you have forsaken me!"

The answer lies not in the simple message but in the hinted message. To explain, let me first help you understand the dynamics of *r'mez* that Jesus is invoking here upon the cross. Imagine one day I am speaking somewhere and a man shouts, "Paul, you bore me and you have an ugly face!" I might simply say in return:

"Sticks and stones, sir, sticks and stones."

Every Englishman knows exactly what I am implying. I am saying the first three words of a well-known children's rhyme:

Sticks and stones may break my bones, but words will never hurt me.

By citing the first line of this familiar saying, I am invoking its whole meaning to my audience. The Englishman realizes that I will not be taking his words to heart.

However, what about the Germans in the room?

Few foreigners know the saying that I have only partially quoted, and so they might interpret my words very differently. They may even create a doctrine based on the importance of standing up for yourself and threatening violence when you are insulted—all based upon my words, "sticks and stones." This is one of the dangers of skimming the surface of Scripture. We come up with 'Biblical' doctrines that may fit into our worldview, but not God's.

When Jesus is on the cross, He is quoting the first verse of Psalm 22.

Now some people may have realized that, but they rarely understand the dynamic that Jesus was using. On the cross, He is not simply quoting a memory verse; He is doing something far more profound. Christ is bringing to life the whole of the Psalm! He is essentially declaring the whole of its message to be true and fulfilled before their eyes. Jesus is invoking *r'mez*.

Psalm 22 starts off with: *'My God, My God, why have you forsaken me?'*

But this poem, which was approximately 1,000 years old at the time of the crucifixion, also includes the following staggering remarks:

> *I am poured out like water, and all my bones are out of joint [...] My mouth is dried up like a potsherd, and my tongue sticks to the roof of my mouth; you lay me in the dust of death. Dogs surround me, a pack of villains encircles me; they pierce my hands and my feet. All my bones are on display; people stare and gloat over me. They divide my clothes among them and cast lots for my garment.* [30]

On the hill at Calvary when Jesus cried out these words, a filtering process occurred. Those simply following the Son of God for the sake of food, healing, and escape from their Roman overlords would have just walked away from that hill disappointed that they did not get from Jesus what they had come to expect.

However, some may have had ears to hear.

How the hairs on their necks must have stood up when they realized that King David's prophecy was coming to pass before their very eyes! Water *was* pouring out of his side as a Roman soldier pierced it with a spear, his bones *were* dislocated as He was raised and lowered on the stake and His clothes *had* been divided among the guards. If they were truly seeking the Kingdom of God, how their hearts would also have beaten faster when Jesus's shout brought to mind what He was really getting at . . . the following verses from the rest of the Psalm:

> *You who fear the Lord, praise him! Revere him, all you descendants of Israel! For he has not despised or scorned the suffering of the afflicted one; he has not hidden his face from him but has listened to his cry for help. [...] All the ends of the earth will remember and turn to the Lord [...] those who cannot keep themselves alive. Posterity will serve him; future generations will be told about the Lord. They will proclaim his righteousness, declaring to a people yet unborn: He has done it!*[31]

He has done it, or, in other words: *"It is finished."*

Jesus was not forsaken!

And He knew it!

All of this would have a greater purpose. It would bring future generations and different nations to Him and change the world as they knew it!

For me, the *implied* meaning challenges my soul. It teaches me a principle as I connect the story of Jesus's death to King David's Psalm. I realize that God is looking for those who will not simply follow Him because He fulfills their individual immediate needs, but instead He longs for those who long for His ultimate, intimate plan. And those who do so will have their individual intimate needs met if they put His plan first.

It also forces me to ask myself the question, "Would I have just walked away thinking, *It's over—this guy is not who I thought he was*?" Or, would my heart have been leaning forward, amazed, intrigued, and excited by the message of Psalm 22?

All of this from one verse that many of us skip over even though deep down we know there's something very odd about it.

Blessed

The *implied* meaning takes many forms, but most of them hint at something unsaid.

When John the Baptist, Jesus's cousin, is in prison, it seems he begins to wrestle with all kinds of doubts about Jesus's identity. At one point, he finally sends some of his disciples to his relative to ask the question:

> *"Are you the one who is to come, or should we expect someone else?"* [32]

Jesus's reply at first seems like a straightforward answer:

> *Jesus replied, "Go back and report to John what you hear and see: The blind receive sight, the lame walk, those who have leprosy are cleansed, the deaf hear, the dead are raised, and the good news is proclaimed to the poor."* [33]

He lists some of His extraordinary acts, but then, He completes it with an enigmatic conclusion:

> *"Blessed is anyone who does not stumble on account of me."* [34]

What does this last phrase have to do with anything? How could John possibly fall away from Jesus? And in what way would he be blessed if he did not?

In Jesus's reply to John's disciples, He is invoking to their minds the seven works that the Jews were expecting of the Messiah based upon the prophecies of Isaiah.

He will make the blind to see. (Isaiah 29:18 & 35:5)

He will make the lame walk. (Isaiah 35:6)

He will cleanse lepers. (Isaiah 53:4)

He will make the deaf hear. (Isaiah 29:18 & 35:5)

He will raise the dead. (Isaiah 11:1-2, implied)[35]

He will evangelize the poor. (Isaiah 61:1)

He will set the prisoners free. (Isaiah 61:1)

These specific miracles were the litmus test or measurement with which the Jews would compare any pseudo-Messiah. The Sanhedrin used this list of seven wonders when sending a posse of religious leaders to check out any claims of candidacy for Messiahship.

Jesus lists the things He has done, but what do you notice?

With *r'mez*, sometimes what you don't say is more powerful than what you do say. What I notice is this: Jesus only points to six of the seven prophetic acts. He leaves out one.

Can you guess which one?

When John's disciples approached, Jesus had already read the heart of the one who sent them. By invoking *r'mez*, Jesus let John know two important things:

Yes, I am the Messiah, but no, I will not be setting you free!

Then He also assured John that if he did not fall away because of the *way in which He does things*, he would be especially blessed.

The *intended* meaning provided the context of the seven prophecies and helped me understand that Jesus was relaying six of Isaiah's prophecies. But, it is only when I understand the *r'mez* that the *implied* meaning communicates God's principle to me: *The Lord puts His Kingdom before my personal concerns.*

He has a plan that I may not understand, but if I also put His Kingdom first, then I can trust that, in the eternal scheme of things, I will also be blessed and given all I really need.

Messiah

R'mez is also a key method used to reveal identity.

It is often argued that Jesus never claimed to be God. Again, those who read but do not study will be particularly vulnerable to that idea. However, if we understand the dynamics of the *implied* level, we will clearly see various claims that Jesus made, not only about Himself but about others also.

> *"Come to me, all you who are weary and burdened, and I will give you rest. Take my yoke upon you and learn from me, for I am gentle and humble in heart, and you will find rest for your souls. For my yoke is easy and my burden is light."* [36]

Jesus was using language that only God would use. It was the wisdom of God, personified in Proverbs, who invited people to come to her, find rest, and accept her yoke. Moreover, *"And I will give you rest"* is a divine claim alluding to Jeremiah 31:25, part of a prophecy that begins with the words, *"At that time,"* declares the Lord, *"I will be the God of all the families of Israel, and they will be my people."* The entire passage that Jesus is invoking is a promise that only God makes to His people. Furthermore, *"I will give you rest"* also reminds the Jews of God's commitment to Moses in Exodus 33:14.

Jesus spoke in a way that only one claiming to be God would speak.

Imagine if this weekend your pastor stood up and told the congregation that he was the way, the truth, and the life and that you could only come to the Father through him! Essentially Jesus, using *r'mez*, did this time and again but we have to understand the dynamic of *r'mez* to fully comprehend some of the claims He was making.

No wonder the religious mafia got so annoyed at Jesus!

But there was another reason . . .

> *But when the chief priests and the teachers of the law saw the wonderful things he did and the children shouting in the temple courts, "Hosanna to the Son of David," they were indignant. "Do you hear what these children are saying?" they asked him. "Yes," replied Jesus, "have you never read, 'From the lips of children and infants you, Lord, have called forth your praise'?"* [37]

Here, Jesus is quoting Psalm 8:2, but again, doing much more than that. He quotes only half of the verse and in doing so uses silence to make a dramatic and powerful statement for all to hear. Listen to the rest of that verse:

> *From the lips of children and infants, you have ordained praise, because of your enemies, to silence the foe and the avenger.* [38]

Using *r'mez*, Jesus declares His attackers to be the very foes of God prophesied by David. Stopping halfway through the verse, He actually uses silence to remind His foes that God will silence them!

And then what He does next makes me laugh. Leaving His words hanging and His audience open mouthed . . . He just walks away.

> *And he left them and went out of the city to Bethany, where he spent the night.* [39]

Jesus dropped the mic!

Stamps

I collect *r'mez* in the same way that some people collect stamps.

Jesus was very good at speaking in parables but uniquely gifted at hinting. An estimated 50 *r'mez* are recorded within Jesus's words in the four Gospels and countless more are in the rest of the Bible. The genius of Jesus is that He was able to say things without saying them. This not only helped Him avoid being trapped by His accusers, but more importantly, it helped those sincerely wishing to be changed by Him to really get what He was communicating.

As we discover more of the *context* of the Bible, so the potential of discovering more *connections* grows. The more connections you can unearth, the more exciting Bible study becomes, especially if you have been a church-going Christian for many years and thought you had already heard everything. Jesus said many things that were only understood later on by His disciples; similarly, there may be things you have read many times before that only now will become clear as you apply the *implied* level.

Like stamps, *r'mez* share an attribute that most of us could emulate:

> They stick to one thing until they get there.

How?

Implication

Why can't the Bible just be simple? Why must its authors and participants hint at things when they could have just come out and said them?

It is because God wants us to find not only the point we need to know for now but also the principle we will need in our future. In light of that, how do we discover these principles and help others find them also?

This second stage analyzes the level of people's perceptions as we look for principles and patterns. A good Haverim group will encourage the genius of making connections. The value of seeing what at first cannot be seen and the struggle to dig deeper than the obvious should be commended.

Again at this level, *specific* and *generic* questions are posed.

The *specific* question should be prompted by the following:

> Is there a pattern to be discovered or a principle to be applied?

If, as the facilitator, I have a principle that I am hoping my friends will discover, then the *specific* question will reflect this. In other words, it will be based around particular aspects of the passage. You will see an example of this on page 108 in the *infrastructure* section titled 'Process.'

The *generic* questions are:

> Does the passage refer to another Scripture, story, or prophecy in the Bible?

> Does anything referenced here have a meaning elsewhere in Scripture?

The *action point* then helps them summarize what they've learned. By making their newfound principle concise and memorable, they will be better able to share it with others. Therefore, the *action point* is:

> Put the principle into a sound bite, diagram, or story to share.

So where do we find these implications in Scripture?

Scriptures

Verses

The most basic form of *r'mez* is cross-referencing. We make a connection to a reference in another part of the Bible, read its context, and see if we can find a hint of a wider message. Some of the *r'mez* I pointed out were ones you could have seen for yourself. They were hidden in the cross-references of most Bibles, but many of us are just not interested enough to check them out because we don't realize the dynamic sometimes being used.

Phrases

Look for a phrase that stands out in the Scripture you are studying. In the same way as Jesus's statement on the cross is found in Psalm 22, does this phrase appear in other places in the Bible? Is one referencing another? An added aspect of this is the law of 'first mention,' which means that if you can find the very first time that verse appears, you may see something at which the writer is hinting.

Names

When a name of a place or a person comes up, see if it is connected to its appearance elsewhere in Scripture. Discover the story behind the other references and explore any hints that may be suggesting a deeper truth. The Scripture you are studying may be brought to life through the context of the Scripture to which it is connected.

Numbers

Most numbers in the Bible have significance. If you notice when Jesus reminds His disciples of the feeding of the 4,000 and 5,000, He points to two specific numbers—not the amount of people fed, but, oddly, the amount of baskets left over. When the feeding of the 5,000 was performed in Galilee, 12 baskets were recovered, yet when in another area, only seven baskets were left over. There is something about these numbers that Jesus felt was important for His disciples to grasp. There was a clue to something they had not yet realized. The *Hasidim* referred to the land where the feeding of 5,000 took place as the land of Israel, but the Hellenistic cities of the Decapolis were referred to as the Land of the Seven. Using a number-based *r'mez*, Jesus is saying to them that He is the bread of life both to the Jews and the Gentiles.

Places

The *implied* meaning can help us see beyond the words and help us sense something of what God actually feels. Not only are the words not said as important as those that are said, but also *where* they are said can have huge implications. Famously, before His arrest, Jesus goes to the Garden of Gethsemane on the Mount of Olives, and during the evening, He utters these incredible words:

> *"Father, if you are willing, take this cup from me; yet not my will, but yours be done."* [40]

There are two *r'mez* in this verse, but I will just share one with you. The six middle words are shocking:

> *". . . yet not my will, but yours . . ."*

This is the only time in the Bible that we see the Son's will as different from the Father's. I had never noticed that until a member of a Haverim group pointed it out. Up until then, maybe because I always knew what happened next, I just thought Jesus was going through the motions. But one *r'mez* brings this passage to life. It adds tension, suspense, and most importantly, a better sense of Jesus's sacrificial state of mind. You see, in the prophecy of Zechariah, it is said that the Mount of Olives will split and the valley that God creates there will be used by the people as an *escape route* from their enemies.[41] It is here, in this chosen place, that Jesus asked to be delivered. Had He gone here to remind His Father of the prophecy? Was Jesus hinting at something? Was it here that Jesus was hoping to escape if the Father willed it? Some might say this is pure coincidence. Is it?

If you have a heart to understand, you will notice that a few moments earlier Jesus had quoted from the predictions of Zechariah:

> *I will strike the shepherd, and the sheep of the flock will be scattered.*[42]

There is no doubt in my mind that this prophecy was on *His* mind. Jesus was not just flippantly going through the motions, requesting something He knew could never happen. This was a genuine request! Jesus had options. He was taken to the very brink of temptation. He really was asking the Father to take His destiny away, but something in the moment stopped Jesus from demanding an alternative path.

Places are significant. Often, there is an implication and a lesson to be learned. In this case, the *implied* meaning helps me see Jesus modeling a principle close to His heart:

> Sometimes we must sacrifice our rights in order to fulfill our responsibilities.

For the *implied* meaning to work, the leader may want to remind those involved of the three things needed. First, the hearer must first know the context. Secondly, they must be spiritually keen enough to make connections. Thirdly, the hearer must actually believe the fuller message for the hint to carry any weight. For instance, if the 'sticks and stones' analogy were ever really used, it would not only fail with those who have never heard the full poem, but also with someone who *does* believe that words *can* harm us (which I of course do).

For the *implied* level to truly change us, it requires two things:

The *faithfulness* to look for a deeper message and the *faith* to believe in it.

Summary

So let me summarize a suggested process for finding *r'mez*.

Like the *intended* level, this *implied* level also uses Bible study resources. To find connections in Scripture that lead to a principle, provide the following *specific* and *generic* questions. After giving time for research, ask the group to share their discoveries. Use the *action point* to prompt each person to summarize a principle from the passage so they can easily share it with others.

Specific Question:

> Is there a pattern to be discovered or a principle to be applied?

Generic Questions:

> Does the passage refer to another Scripture, story, or prophecy in the Bible?

> Does anything referenced here have a meaning elsewhere in Scripture?

Action Point:

> Put this principle into a sound bite, diagram, or story to share.

INTERPRETED

D'rash | Collaboration | Purpose

Why?

Space

Imagine a life in which you have the freedom to grasp the purpose God has for you.

"Other seed fell among thorns, which grew up and choked the plants."[43]

The thorns tell us of those who are excited, enthused, and even idealistic. The message of the Kingdom becomes their vision as well. Over time, however, other dreams come in that take over. The more seductive temptations of stuff, status, and security. The mission may remain; it is rarely discarded, but there is not enough space in their lives to let the seed grow beyond a weak and withered shoot. The growth they had is stunted.

Ever felt that your understanding of God's Word was stifled?

Ever felt that your religion lacked space to pursue God's purposes?

Maybe there is a connection.

Some of us are bored with the Word of God because all we hear are the same old clichés. I have often wondered: Where are the *deeper* explanations? Where is the gap for *innovative* applications?

He said to them, "Therefore every teacher of the law who has become a disciple in the kingdom of heaven is like the owner of a house who brings out of his storeroom new treasures as well as old."[44]

Will there ever be room for *new* interpretations to complement the *old* ones? Or are they destined to attack each other for all time?

I believe we need to rediscover a Biblical way to collaborate.

It has been said that a parable compares something familiar to something unfamiliar, the familiar being material and the unfamiliar being spiritual. Jesus would point to something everyone understood in order to explain something they did not yet understand.

The problem is that every one of us sees the world slightly different, and therefore the spiritual world slightly differently as well. But is that really a problem? Or is it actually an opportunity?

We all see from different angles.

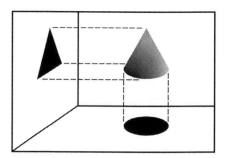

Take a look at the diagram above. From one perspective, all you can see is a triangle; from another, all that is recognized is a circle. Not until both perspectives are united is the recognition of a full cone seen by all. Now look at this second illustration:

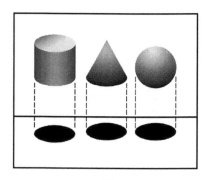

Three very different objects are viewed from only one perspective. This singular viewpoint dumbs down the variety, objectivity, and possibility of what is really there. The idea that one man or woman should speak and interpret Scripture for everyone will always hamstring our potential as a community to see the fullness of the Kingdom.

The third level of Haverim Devotions will teach us how to avoid just that. It will help us find the *collaboration* required to comprehend God's *purpose* in a passage—not because that one perspective is necessarily wrong; it may be just terribly incomplete.

The sages said, "Every scripture has seventy facets."[45]

Seventy is the number that represents infinity. In other words, there are an infinite number of truths to discover in the Bible. Please understand that I am not promoting pluralism but perspective. Of course there are dangers in this, as I will discuss later, but authentic study must take this risk. In the days of Jesus, it *always did*, and in our emerging world, it *always must*.

In doing so, Haverim can move us away from *one-to-many* to *many-to-many* and help us become inclusive rather than exclusive. We can build a community that is less polarized and invite some unusual travelers along the way—ones who could not journey with us in our old vehicle because they were at best passengers, but who can now become participators.

Together we can all gain spiritual depth perception.

What?

Collaboration

The third level of Haverim Devotions is the *interpreted* meaning.

The *interpreted* meaning offers perspectives that fill the gaps in a passage.

The Hebrew word for this level is *d'rash* and means 'search.'

The method of the *interpreted* meaning is to seek *collaboration* in order to discover the *purpose*.

To go to this next level, more than asking questions, we become the question. We engage ourselves in the passage by embedding ourselves within it. *D'rash* was an ancient way of interpreting a passage by filling in the gaps. It brings together what is familiar to each one of us in order to see what is unfamiliar to every one of us.

If *r'mez* is where we let Scripture interpret Scripture, *d'rash* is where Scripture interprets motive. Before, we simply read the Bible; now the Bible reads us. In doing so, it helps us understand our hopes and fears, His hopes and dreams.

If we miss the *collaboration*, we may miss His *purpose*—not because we cannot find purpose, but because we only see it from one angle . . . usually our own.

When we examine a passage at this level, we discover the motive behind what was said or done by creating our *d'rash*, which was a compelling form of interpretation practiced by the sages when they expanded on a Biblical text.[46] In order to both gain and give insight, they would often inject themselves into the narrative. I have developed a simple format from this practice so we can benefit from this ancient method.

The *interpreted* passage is, for some, the most dynamic and freeing of all four levels. It appeals especially to those who love learning not just about God, but others. And, it creates an adventure of unlimited possibilities. At the *interpreted* level, we can also discover more about what limits our relationship with God and what could take it to a new level.

Rather than me teaching you the lessons I have learned from this level, let me help you learn your own.

Jehoash

Do you fully use all that is at your disposal?

If not, why not?

Within the Bible is a story of King Jehoash—not a very godly man, but a man who knew God.[47] He is facing the king of Aram and realizes that defeat is inevitable. In the course of a strange story, a prophet asks the king to perform two bizarre activities.

First, he asks him to shoot an arrow through a window, and then he tells him to strike the ground with the arrows. The king, for reasons it does not say, only strikes the ground *three* times. The prophet, again for reasons not mentioned, is annoyed at the king, and after promising a full victory, now instead proclaims only a *half* victory.

Have you ever felt that you only get half-victories? Do you sometimes only half-heartedly use what God has given you? Why is that?

To help us understand his motive more fully, let me take you through the process of *d'rash*. To do this, we first look at the *intended* and *implied* levels, the *context* and the *connections*.

The *context* teaches me that Jehoash was an ungodly man, and that he was facing the King of Aram with what *The NIV Study Bible* describes as a 'small police force' for an army. He had inherited only 10 chariots, 50 horsemen, and 10,000 soldiers. Bear in mind that in 857 BC, Ahab had destroyed 10 times as many foot soldiers in one day of battle!

Secondly, context teaches us the meaning of Jehoash's statement when he met with the prophet Elisha:

> *"My father, my father, the chariots and horsemen of Israel!"*[48]

This also may seem like one of those peculiar phrases we skip because we don't understand. However, it has significance to the story.

Ancient Hebrews describe things differently from those in the modern western world. When we describe something, we usually comment on its decorative state, but the ancient Hebrews would describe something by its *function*. Even when a color was mentioned, it was symbolic because the color itself had a function. I, as an Englishman, may describe a sofa from IKEA as white and contemporary, whereas an ancient Hebrew might describe it as sturdy and with space to seat three people.[49]

So when Jehoash approaches Elisha, he greets the prophet by declaring his *function*. He has realized that Elisha represents Israel's only significant military resource.

The *connections* are where we go next. When the prophet commands the king to shoot an arrow through the east window, he is *hinting* in advance to Jehoash the possibility of more than just a simple victory. He is using *r'mez* by invoking into the king's memory an ancient practice of declaring war.

In history, when one faction felt offended or aggrieved by another, it would sometimes declare an intention to go to war by throwing a spear or shooting an arrow into the enemy's territory. This signified 30 days for the enemy to put things right and avoid conflict.

Here we may discover a helpful principle implied elsewhere in Scripture.[50] How do we know when a Godly influence comes into our lives? We know because it moves us from defense to attack!

So the story is that Jehoash, an ungodly man, recognizes the prophet as God's resource and understands that God is giving him an opportunity to move from a position of desperation to one of advancement. So, why is it that the following happens?

> Then he said, "Take the arrows," and the king took them. Elisha told him, "Strike the ground." He struck it three times and stopped. The man of God was angry with him and said, "You should have struck the ground five or six times; then you would have defeated Aram and completely destroyed it. But now you will defeat it only three times."[51]

To understand what was going on in the heart of Jehoash, I first told you the story, and then gave you context. Now let me give you the verse and question.

Please look at 2 Kings 13:18:

> Then he said, "Take the arrows," and the king took them. Elisha told him, "Strike the ground." He struck it three times and stopped.

The question is:

> Why did Jehoash only strike the ground three times?

To discover the lessons for yourself, I invite you to:

> Retell the story, fill in the gaps, but whatever you do, don't change the facts.

In no more than three sentences, I would like you to write the story from Jehoash's point of view. It is important that you write in first person. So for instance, "I picked up the arrows" not "he picked up the arrows."

You need to tell us what you were thinking when Elisha gave you the command. What was going on in your mind and heart when you struck the ground?

Please write your *d'rash* on the lines that follow.

_____

_____

_____

_____

Warning: It is *very* important that you do this exercise before you read on. If you skip this, you will lose the power of what is about to happen.

So, what conclusion did you arrive at? What was going on in Jehoash's mind? What was he feeling in his heart? Why did he recognize God's resource, but not use it to its fullest?

Based upon what you just wrote, what is your summary of Jehoash's reason for not striking the ground three more times? Was it that he needed more instructions? Was it because he didn't know why and didn't see the point? Was it because no one told him he could strike the ground more than three times? Was it because he was impatient to finish this bit of nonsense so that the prophet would quickly give him the real answer to his problem?

There are two benefits to this exercise.

First, if you were doing this in a Haverim, the combined perspectives give a fuller understanding of why people, including your friends, don't use all at their disposal.

Secondly, and perhaps more significantly, according to the ancient rabbis and sages before and after Jesus's day, what you wrote is the *possible* reason that Jehoash did not use God's resource, but it is the *probable* reason why you would not have!

Importantly, the rabbis are not suggesting that you would have done what Jehoash did; rather, if you had, then this is probably why. The benefit of understanding your motive in this 'virtual reality' is that you can then prepare yourself for real situations you may face.

Is that true for you? When you look at your *d'rash*, does it help you understand why you don't use all that God puts at your disposal?

This ancient process helps us engage in the story in a way unfamiliar to most of us. It gives us the freedom to explore and is particularly engaging for those who may not know God in the way you do, because as long as the *p'shat* is not compromised, there is no right or wrong answer . . . only perspective.

Peter

Let us look at the positive side of this exercise by asking, do you ever step out in faith?

If yes, why?

> *Immediately Jesus made the disciples get into the boat and go on ahead of him to the other side, while he dismissed the crowd [. . .] and the boat was already a considerable distance from land, buffeted by the waves because the wind was against it. Shortly before dawn, Jesus went out to them, walking on the lake. When the disciples saw him walking on the lake, they were terrified. "It's a ghost," they said, and cried out in fear. But Jesus immediately said to them: "Take courage! It is I. Don't be afraid."*[52]

As you know, Peter then stepped out of the boat.

You may have stepped out in the past, maybe you are doing so right now, yet sometimes maybe you have not. What can you learn about the times you have stepped out that could help you in the future? Could immersing ourselves in that story help us understand what would give us faith to do what Peter did in other areas of our lives? Let's find out!

First, let me give you the verse and question.

Please look at Matthew 14:28-29:

> *"Lord, if it's you," Peter replied, "tell me to come to you on the water."*
>
> *"Come," he said.*
>
> *Then Peter got down out of the boat, walked on the water and came toward Jesus.*

Then answer the question:

> Why did Peter step out of the boat?

Now, in first person and in no more than three sentences, rewrite the story, fill in the gaps, but whatever you do, don't change the facts.

_____

_____

_____

_____

_____

_____

What did you see?

Did Peter do it because his friends encouraged him to? Was it because he was in the habit of always walking towards Jesus? Did he do it just to prove the miraculous to those watching?

Whatever you wrote is a *possible* reason why Peter stepped out of the boat, but the *probable* reason why you would have. Whatever the reason may be, your discoveries can empower you for the future. When you want to step out in some area of your life, you can make sure you put into place the things you now know will lift your levels of faith.

Wrestle

At its most dynamic, the *interpreted* level is an exercise in theology, not anthropology.[53]

Being part of a Haverim will provoke your mind and challenge your heart to learn so many new things about yourself and your friends, but that is not its primary motive. What floats my boat is the idea that you and I can learn to grasp what is in the heart of God and know Him more closely.

Recently, a member of my Haverim asked if we could look at the story of Jacob wrestling with a man of God. They wondered what this enigmatic story was all about and hoped it could teach us about our struggles with the Lord. For me, it represented an opportunity to explore what is in God's heart and mind when He forces us to wrestle instead of just teaching us clearly the lesson we need to learn.

During the first two stages, we discovered where Jacob was, what was going through his mind, quite a lot about his nature and history, and we came to different conclusions of who the man of mystery was that fought Jacob. However, instead of slipping into the story as Jacob, we put ourselves in the place of God Himself.

I gave the following Scripture:

> So Jacob was left alone, and a man wrestled with him till daybreak.[54]

Then I asked the following question:

> Why did God ask the angel to specifically wrestle with Jacob—why not ask him to simply speak to Jacob or instruct him through an illustrative miracle?

To do this, I gave them the following simple exercise:

> Write a letter from God to the angel telling him your thoughts on Jacob and why specifically you want him to fight with Jacob.

Again, they put themselves in first person and kept their letter to around three sentences. The first sentence contained what they thought about Jacob, the second was exactly what they instructed the angel to do, and the third described what they hoped would be the benefit of the wrestling contest.

What would your *d'rash* be?

_____

_____

_____

_____

_____

_____

_____

_____

We found two benefits to this exercise.

First, our Haverim began to learn from each other's experiences a little more of why God brought those people we struggle with into our lives. Secondly, we learned from the perspective of other people something about God's heart that may not have occurred to us if we had simply tackled this story on our own.

Knowing God and knowing ourselves . . . two of the most important discoveries in life.

How?

Interpretation

So how do we lead ourselves and others as we create our own *d'rash*?

This third level takes on a different feel from the first two in that it empha-sizes *relationship* rather than *research*. Another unique aspect is that it primarily uses instructions rather than questions. Yet it is an overarching question that guides the process, searching for the underlying purpose:

> What was going on in the character's heart and mind?

At this level we are looking for a motive; therefore, when choosing our specific question, we are prompted by what seems unclear about the *reason* something was done or not done by someone. That might mean looking for the purpose behind God's actions or words. Alternatively, it could mean looking at the reason people acted or spoke the way they did.

The *specific* instructions are:

> Choose the character and verse(s) to interpret and ask why they did what they did.

After determining what our specific question will be, we can then move through the following process.

The *generic* instructions are:

> Rewrite the verse(s) in first person.
> Include what the character may have been thinking or feeling.

Retell the story, fill in the gaps, but whatever you do, don't change the facts.

During this process, we allow time for the group members to put themselves in the story and rewrite the verse *in first person*. This is key as it puts us into the character's position in a more meaningful way. So again, not "She did . . ." but "I did . . ." Not "He thought to himself . . ." but "I thought to myself . . ." If you do not include that dynamic, you will find this level to be less powerful.

Some important tips here:

Firstly, when I lead this level in a Haverim, I find it helpful to ask people to be completely quiet and not discuss it with each other; in this way, they can focus without distractions.

Secondly, when interpreting a passage, do not *d'rash* all of it. Instead, choose a key verse or short section on which you believe the meaning hinges. A *d'rash* should be only one to three sentences long. The shorter it is, the more insightful it tends to be.

Thirdly, encourage the group members to write down what first comes to mind. Do not overthink your interpretation if you want to discover what you *really* think or believe. The goal is not the cleverest interpretation, but the most authentic and revealing one.

The *action point* that follows is simple:

Read out your *d'rash* and optionally use a creative tool to explain what you discovered.

Each person should read their version of the verse verbatim. If they simply tell it from the top of their heads, they will often waffle or detour from their initial meditation, which detracts from what can be learned at this level. This ancient dynamic requires that a *d'rash* be written down simply, briefly, and clearly and then read out word for word.

Make sure you take time to discuss the *motive* or purpose that it uncovers. Give space for people to share how they can apply what they discover. Our hope is that, at the end of the exercise, we and our friends will have gained more understanding of God's heart rather than simply His words and actions. We also hope to be empowered in the future by understanding more of what motivates us.

A final tip is that, as the leader, I share my *d'rash* only after the others have shared theirs so that it does not influence their version.

Note to leaders: If you want your members to discover certain truths, you can fill in the gaps in their understanding at this point. For instance, a Haverim may be one of many going through a topic or passage as part of a wider teaching series. In this case, there may be certain spiritual principles or practices that the leadership hopes to teach. This would be a good place to do that. However, remember, the main success of Haverim Devotions is that it is a participation tool, not a presentation tool. Therefore, any teaching must be concise, highlighting just the essentials that they may not have discovered by themselves.

No matter how you use this level, above all, avoid the mistake of sharing *d'rash* without taking the time to discuss how the insights can be applied to people's lives.

Creativity

The simple written exercise that I took you through in the last chapter is powerful enough, but the option of giving people another creative way they can do this is helpful. No matter how good something is, if it is repeatedly done with no variation, it can become cliché. Early on in the life of a Haverim, you may wish to simply have the members read out their *d'rash*; however, giving people a creative way to share what they discovered can keep things fresh and varied.

So what kind of exercises might be used? And does this work for all types of Scripture, including its letters, poems, and prophecies?

Here are just a few examples of the types of exercises we use to *d'rash* a passage.

Art

An alternative to simply writing is to create a form of art. At times I have asked people to draw the story on a piece of paper. After first having everyone write their *d'rash*, my wife has given out paper clips and asked people to manipulate them into a shape that depicts what the person may be thinking or feeling. With a more artistic approach, it is still important for people to retell the story using the method of *d'rash*. However, the practice of including some form of art brings variety and helps those who feel they don't have a way with words.

Drama

In a similar way, the retelling can take the form of a simple skit. Depending on the type of group you are working with, you may find this to be a fun and surprisingly revealing way of gaining perspective on a passage of Scripture.

Many years ago, a school allowed me to teach their drama group on ways that drama communicates philosophy. I spoke about modern films; we watched movie clips and discussed how every producer and director is using art to communicate his or her way of thinking. Then I divided the class into groups and gave them each a parable to read, the point of its intended meaning (such as 'you reap what you sow'), a setting in which it had to take place (such as a bus stop or police station), and one object they had to include. I then instructed them to rewrite the parable in this modern setting in a way that revealed the motives of the characters. They were not allowed to divulge the point, but the rest of the class had to guess what it was.

I did this many times and was repeatedly shocked by how the Holy Spirit led these young people to understand the dynamics of what Jesus had been teaching.

By immersing themselves in the Word, they had engaged themselves with its Author.

Photography

In the western world at least, almost everyone has a camera on their phone. So, for a fairly shy and perhaps initially hesitant group, a photographic approach may open up hearts and minds. A group could be given a few minutes to create their *d'rash* privately. Then, when they have realized what is in the heart of a character, they could simply take a photo of something that best represents it.

When the Haverim regroups, they can show the photo to everyone and either explain why they took it or allow the group to guess the meaning. This latter option creates a two-tiered approach to interpretation that can be doubly effective.

Game

Sometimes simple games can be employed. Once I have told a story, I retell it, but this time I leave blanks and point to people in the room who must promptly fill in the gaps. If they take too long or repeat something already said, they are 'out.' Specifically, the gaps that I leave are either something that is said, thought, or believed. The gaps represent things not already contained in the passage. For instance, I may retell the parable of the prodigal son employing gaps like this:

> There was a man who had two sons. The younger son thought to himself _____ and so said to his father, 'Father, give me my share of the estate.' So the man divided his property between his sons, saying to his wife _____. Not long after that . . .

At each blank, I would point to a Haverim member and they would have to quickly respond. This is great once people have understood how the *interpreted* level works, because it gets their immediate response. It does not give them time to coach their thinking or feelings.

Comic

If you have time to prepare, then perhaps one of the most straightforward and easiest ways to get people to 'fill in the gaps' is to create a comic strip like the ones found in a newspaper. This does not have to be elaborate, but could simply be stick figures with blank speech and thought bubbles over their heads. Quite literally, the Haverim members would fill in the thoughts or words. The comic strip can then be handed out on a worksheet or displayed on a TV screen. Very simple, but equally effective.

Literature

This may sound simple enough so far, but how do you *d'rash* something that is not a story?

I will share more thoughts and ideas on this in the Infrastructure section of this book. For now, however, let me say this: If the passage you want to look at is more of a theological statement, a proclamation, a verse of poetry, or some other form of literature, then a simple answer is to step back and create a 'story' about the passage or an incident based upon it. This week for instance, we *d'rashed* Jesus's words to His disciples:

> *"I no longer call you servants, because a servant does not know his master's business. Instead, I have called you friends, for everything that I learned from my Father I have made known to you."* [55]

We wanted to discover at what point Jesus may have realized His disciples were not simply His colleagues, but those He saw as intimate friends. Also, what implications did that have for us?

The specific question I presented was:

> If you were Jesus, at what point in the three-year discipleship process did you see the disciples as your friends?

Then I gave them a piece of paper on which to chart Jesus's companionship with the 12 disciples. They plotted what they considered to be key moments in the story of their relationship and presented a graph that showed the peaks and troughs. Near the bottom of the page was a dotted line representing 'servants' and near the top a similar line representing 'friends.' They then reported their findings, including the point at which they felt the relationship broke through to friendship.

For me, it was particularly revealing as I noticed the possibility that Jesus was friends with some of them before they became disciples and that the discipleship paradigm of the day may have affected that relationship. It made me aware of the profound change in relationship when someone I care about joins Pais and becomes a member of my staff. I learned things from my chart about my heart and about God's heart from my friends' charts.

This stepping back can be done with anything and any passage; it just takes a little extra thought.

Important: I do understand the real fears of this type of engagement in Scripture, but the safety net of the *intended* meaning has proven invaluable. It has amazed me how rarely people misinterpret Scripture or, more accurately, how, when they do, the Spirit leads them back to its simple, straightforward meaning.

Summary

So let me summarize a suggested process for creating *d'rash*.

At this level, we insert ourselves into Scripture in order to reveal a motive. To determine which character and verses to interpret (*d'rash*), decide in advance if you want to gain perspective into the human heart or into God's heart. Once you choose the character, tailor your specific question to the passage by asking 'why', as in 'Why did Jehoash strike the ground only three times?' (Human perspective.) Or, 'Why did God instruct the angel to wrestle with Jacob?' (God's perspective.) Using the *specific* and *generic* instructions, allow 5 to 10 minutes of silence for each person to complete the exercise. Then give the *action point* to encourage people to share their interpretations with the group. Provide time to collaborate on how these interpretations can be applied.

Specific Instructions:

> Choose the character and verse(s) to interpret and ask why they did what they did.

Generic Instructions:

Rewrite the verse(s) in first person.
Include what the character may have been thinking or feeling.
Retell the story, fill in the gaps, but whatever you do, don't change the facts.

Action Point:

Read out your *d'rash* and optionally use a creative tool to explain what you discovered.

Leadership Option:

Briefly fill in the gaps in their understanding with teaching you prepared in advance.

INSPIRED

S'od | Contemplation | Practice

Why?

Soil

Imagine a time when you can thrive in the practice of God's Word.

> *"Still other seed fell on good soil, where it produced a crop—a hundred, sixty or thirty times what was sown."*[56]

The good soil in the Parable of the Soils represents those who hear the exact same message as the other three, yet the seed sown in them grows and flourishes. The reason they produce fruit is not because things are easier or their lives less full. According to Jesus, what makes them good soil for the multiplication of God's Word is . . . understanding. The message they received is expedited.

Ever felt that the gift of God's Word was given to you for others?

Ever felt that your religion was meant to go further?

Maybe there is a connection.

With a new revelation comes a new responsibility, but you may find the thought of sharing God's Word difficult. Even though you want the knowledge to be multiplied, you lack the understanding of how to transfer your faith in a complex world with people who need answers that you don't have.

The benefit of being part of a Haverim is that it provides a place to practice this.

It is important that the Haverim is trained to not only listen for God's voice, but to discern what is and is not from Him. Plus, they should learn how to intelligently apply or pass on what is revealed.

The Spirit and stupidity are a dangerous mix . . . like the man who chose the moment we were both in the gentlemen's restroom to tell me, "Paul, I had a dream about you last night!" Or like the group of young missionaries who, after believing God had given them a message for a disabled man, chased a terrified peg-legged stranger through a carnival screaming at the top of their lungs, "But we have a message from God for you!"

"Stupid is as stupid does."[57]

After becoming a Christian in my early teens, I went to a church that trained its members each week in how to hear from God and share with others what we heard. It was probably the most balanced teaching I have ever heard on the subject. Perhaps the best advice I was given might be summed up like this:

The Holy Spirit will never contradict *His* Word . . . or *yours*.

He will not inspire you to do something that goes against the teaching of the Bible, nor will He encourage you to violate His character within you. It is that kind of wisdom that helps us and this type of accountability that is needed.

The *inspired* level is used, therefore, to create space for God to make His Word specific to our situation and to that of our friends. It is a time to share what we believe God has revealed to us through the passage and to pass on any revelation that we believe will be beneficial to others. At this level, we can experience God speaking to us and through us with the accountability of a group of friends and a safe place to practice.

In our Haverim, we have a mixture of people from different backgrounds. Avoiding denominational sound bites and terms has been useful. When it comes to this fourth level, we have not pushed any particular denominational stance. We just create space for the *contemplation* required to comprehend God's *practices*.

Wouldn't it give you courage to have wise words drop into your head when you were feeling out of your depth? Wouldn't it be inspiring to be given a word that unlocks your heart or someone else's? Wouldn't it give you security to step out into the unknown if you knew the unknown was a little more knowable than you thought?

With greater revelation comes greater opportunity . . . and a greater need to practice.

What?

Contemplation

The fourth level of Haverim Devotions is the *inspired* meaning.

The *inspired* meaning reveals the practices we can apply from a passage.

The Hebrew word for this level is *s'od* and it means 'secret.'

The method of the *inspired* meaning is to seek *contemplation* that reveals a *practice*.

More than any other New Testament writer, the Apostle Paul referred to his revelation of the Messiah as a *s'od*. It is with this *inspired* meaning that Paul says he found his calling.[58] English Bibles translate the concept of *s'od* as 'mystery.'[59]

If *r'mez* is where Scripture interprets Scripture, then *s'od* is where the *Spirit* interprets Scripture.

Here, for the first time, revelation *precedes* research. In other words, we listen for God's voice and, through study, test to see if we heard correctly.

Only when something becomes specific does it become truly dynamic. During our meditations with our Haverim, we can train ourselves to hear God's voice on a passage. We create a place and space where God can speak *to* and *through* us. Scripture and Spirit combine to bring a dynamism that we may have never previously experienced.

If we miss the *contemplation*, we miss His *practices*—not because we do not know what God will do, but because we have already decided in advance how He will do it.

At this level, we ask for understanding. Then, we wait and listen.

We ask God for a word, key verse, or revelation from the Scripture that will be useful to another person also. We ask the same questions we have just asked, but we ask for them. Then those thoughts we receive are either written down and passed to someone on paper or spoken aloud to the group. They can be verbalized or visualized.

The *inspired* level can be the scariest and most challenging to the Haverim, but it has the power to create a defining moment where our lives can change forever.

I once heard of a preacher who, at the beginning of his sermon, confessed the following:

> *"I am so sorry, everybody, but this week I've been busy with funerals and such, so this morning I will just have to rely on the Holy Spirit. Next week, however, I promise to be much better prepared."*

As humorous as this may be, his Freudian slip allows some of us an insight into our own heart and minds. The Holy Spirit is not a dove. He is not a pigeon or a parrot. He is the third person of the Trinity. To be *so* prepared that we are prepared to live life without Him may be to cut and never paste God into our lives. We all need to harness His power for the long haul. Just like gasoline, the Holy Spirit can simply create a dramatic one-off explosion or be welcomed in to run our spiritual engine. In the same way, Haverim presents the opportunity for more than an event, but rather a constant, ongoing infilling.

Wish

Have you ever wished for something?

I have.

So did Moses.

In fact, our wish is exactly the same. You see, the power of the Holy Spirit flows through the whole of the Bible, but we notice a significant difference between His input in the Old Testament and that in the New Testament. Pre-Pentecost, the incidents of the Holy Spirit filling man were occasional and sporadic. He was only poured out for a specific instance, and then He left.

> *Then the Lord came down in the cloud and spoke with him [Moses], and he took some of the power of the Spirit that was on him and put it on the seventy elders. When the Spirit rested on them, they prophesied—but did not do so again.* [60]

Four verses later, Moses wished his wish:

> *"...I wish that all the LORD's people were prophets and that the LORD would put his Spirit on them!"* [61]

Two thousand years later, Moses's request was granted. On the birthday of the Church, God's Spirit began to be poured out permanently and for all time.

But significantly, in both cases, the Holy Spirit cannot be stored up. His power must be used at the time of supply so we can be regularly replenished. I wonder if Moses would have ever imagined a situation like we have today where God *has* poured out His Spirit on all people, but not all of us are taking advantage of having Him.

Moses would turn in his grave . . . if he had one.

Washing

When God's message becomes *specific*, it becomes *dynamic*. More than simply encouraging me, it has empowered me.

Here are some ways that this level of Haverim has shaped my thoughts and my life.

One very simple yet profound episode happened a long time before I had any thoughts at all about the Pais Movement. As I was reading and praying with friends, one of them turned to me and said:

> "Paul, God has a purpose for you, but it will be like a washing line. A washing line is of no use hung from one pole; it has to be hung between two to do its job."

That short observation, this 'word from God,' meant absolutely nothing to me at the time.

Four years later, I was a solo schools worker in North Manchester finding many young people who wanted to know more about the Gospel. One day, while wondering how to connect them into the wider family of God, I read this passage:

> *When he had finished speaking, he said to Simon, "Put out into deep water, and let down the nets for a catch." Simon answered, "Master, we've worked hard all night and haven't caught anything. But because you say so, I will let down the nets." When they had done so, they caught such a large number of fish that their nets began to break.* [62]

Or as *The Message* puts it:

> *. . . straining the nets past capacity.*

Immediately the question dropped into my mind:

> *Paul, if you were one of the disciples and you knew a week before that this was going to happen . . . what would you do?*

It was almost a rhetorical question because instantly the answer also hit me:

> I would spend the week building the biggest net I could!

Then came the impression . . .

> *Go do it.*

But how?

It was as though God had already given me the understanding four years previously. He had laid the foundation as to how I should apply that passage . . . *Partnership*.

A year later, I founded the first Pais Project team. Since then, I have often felt the pressure and expectations of the unique 'washing line' system we had created whereby our apprentices served both a local church and worked for Pais as an organization. Yet this *s'od*, this revelation that preceded the problem, this concept that came from the Spirit not my wisdom, has brought me great peace, assuring me we are on the right track. As I reflect 20 years later, I am also reminded that the tension created between serving both a local church and Pais led to the creativity required to reach schools where others had previously failed.

The Spirit *does* wash our brain, not with a desire to wipe its imagination, but with a passion to cleanse it from worldly paradigms.

On many other occasions, I have found that, if I give God the space to speak, He will give me a flow of creativity that I cannot and should not realistically expect.

When I am preparing a message, writing a book, or developing a new strategy and have a creative block, I have now learned to stop, take my fingers off the keyboard, and walk up and down my study singing and praising God in the Spirit. I can honestly say that I can only remember one incident in the last few years where that productive void was not filled within a couple minutes, if not seconds, with fresh insight, ideas, and even artistry.

Writer's block is not due to a lack of substance, but a lack of space.

Flower

Many years later, a similar episode to the 'washing line' word happened.

In my book *The Kingdom Patterns*, I unpack the idea of finding God's direction in life.[63] Instead of the typical questions of, 'Where should I go? Who should I follow? What should I do?' I propose a different one based on Jesus's words on the mountain:

"But seek first his kingdom and his righteousness . . ."[64]

The question that I use to find God's will is:

What will most advance the Kingdom of God?

When seeking direction, this question rarely lets me down. Sometimes, however, I need extra help from the Holy Spirit. One major case came when I was leading a church in the UK but was asked to immigrate to the USA in order to create an international base for Pais. This particular day, when asking my usual question, it occurred to me that although I loved both things, Pais and the church I pastored, Pais was my *favorite* because it had by far the greatest impact.

I had included the church in my journey from the moment I began taking the request from Texas seriously. Yet I was very surprised when one day, a particularly supportive lady in the church, one who really wanted me to stay, said she felt the Holy Spirit had put a message on her heart for me:

"Paul, the Lord says you must pick your favorite flower and plant it in a place where it would not normally flourish."

The use of the word 'favorite' was specific, and so the message became dynamic.

The words God gave her for me were probably partly for her as well. It was revelation to her and confirmation to me.

Just as there are many types of *r'mez* and facets of *d'rash*, so there are many variations of *s'od*. The ones I have written about are just a couple of examples. The Spirit may not speak within the actual Haverim meeting; that's not really the point of it. The purpose of our getting together is to prepare us to hear Him while we are chatting with our friends, neighbors, colleagues, and the strangers we meet along the way. As I once heard a colleague put it, "I do not pray every morning to hear The Holy Spirit during that time; I pray every morning so I can hear God whilst eating pizza in the evening."

In the same way, Haverim becomes a training ground for what happens outside of it.

Axe

The Spirit plus space equals sharpness.

There is a story told of a young, jobless lumberjack desperate to feed his new family. Approaching a logging company, he begged the foreman for employment but was told no positions were available. The young man was so distressed and concerned about his wife and two small children that, after further pleading, the foreman agreed to give him a four-week trial. During it, the hopeful father worked harder than anyone else, and yet at the end of the first week, he was called into the boss's office and fired!

He was told he had started well, but as the week progressed, he had chopped down fewer and fewer trees. Stunned and confused, he implored the foreman to give him one more chance, stating that he had worked every moment possible. He explained that he even labored through the morning and lunchtime breaks, still chopping at trees while the others rested.

The foreman raised his eyebrows, paused, and asked the lumberjack to give him his axe. Carefully and meticulously, he glided his fingers along the edge of its blade, and then put it down. With a slight smile, he instructed the young man with the following words:

> "I now see the problem. When the other workers take a break, they spend their time not only eating and resting, but sharpening their axes as well. You have not, so your axe is blunt, and that is why you proved such an ineffective employee."

A lesson was learned, and the job offer continued.

The *inspired* level of Haverim Devotions helps us sharpen our spiritual axes.

How?

Inspired

I have found that *community* builds *competence*.

So how do I explore all that God has for me at this level, plus lead others through their contemplations?

We ask a mixture of *personal* questions and *friendship* questions.

The *personal* questions we first ask for ourselves are:

> Lord, what do I not yet understand about this passage?
> What has previously been hidden to me?
> What do You want me to do in response to this passage?

Then we ask God for a word, key verse, illustration, or revelation from the Scripture that will be useful to another person in our Haverim, the entire group, or someone else in our community.

Our *friendship* questions are therefore prompted by the following:

> Is there someone to whom I can pass on a message from this passage and how should I do that?

Any thoughts we receive can either be written down and passed on paper or spoken aloud to the group. It is important to remember that the primary objective is not to hear God there and then, although this can of course be a huge benefit. The point is to keep listening for His voice during the rest of our week.

The *action point* then follows:

> If appropriate, share what God said to you and what He inspired you to tell others.

Haverim may not be the moment we receive great answers, but it can be the moment we ask the great questions that lead to us receiving great answers at another time.

So how can we help people listen for His voice?

Catalyst

As I have mentioned, one of the benefits of Haverim is the attraction to postmoderns. A culture that wants to *experience*, *participate*, *imagine*, and *connect* is greatly helped when we no longer see Bible study as a one sensory encounter. Good Haverim facilitators will take time to think through the setting in which this level is undertaken. Simply dimming lights, lighting candles, and working hard to make sure that distracting noises are limited can greatly enhance the experience.

Yet, there is more.

The following are some suggestions of different things you can do as a catalyst to reflection if you are in a group setting. I am not suggesting that you do all of them or that you even have to use any of them for this level to be successful. All I would say is that variety is the spice of life and a catalyst can help the Holy Spirit focus people's attention in a similar way the burning bush did for Moses. Use them if they do the same for you, but do not use them if you find yourself or others focusing on the creative tool rather than the Scripture itself.

Mosaics

Many years ago, while teaching lessons in public schools, I learned the importance of what we at Pais call 'mosaics,' the use of various fragments to give a fuller picture. It is true to say that those who advance the Kingdom of God are the ones who go the extra mile, and so rather than turning up five minutes before a class was about to start, our habit was to arrive much earlier to recreate the room with permission from the teacher. We found that familiarity is an enemy of faith, and that even by moving the chairs and tables around to create a different setting, we created anticipation. A sense that something was about to happen hung in the air, and in my opinion, stirring anticipation is the first step to encouraging the faith needed to expect something new.

One of the first times we did this was on a lesson about forgiveness. Wanting to emphasize the negative impact of bitterness, the song *Don't Look Back in Anger* by Oasis was playing as the students entered the class, giving them a chance to focus on that topic as we prepared them for the lesson. We also had games where students would bite into particularly sour citrus fruit. We used smell, sight, sound, and touch to help them get the message.

A Haverim leader will do well to copy the idea that we had and create anticipation by involving the senses in the *s'od* experience. I am in no way saying that at the fourth stage of Haverim we need to create a Broadway theater production; in fact, that would work against the whole idea of providing space. I'm simply encouraging you to put a little extra thought into the exercise in order to help people get started.

Sight

When we begin our contemplations, I sometimes use visual aids as a catalyst. This is a delicate and finely balanced skill because we want participants to focus on the passage or verse, not the image in front of them. The images should not take away from the passage but form a backdrop to help focus prayer and intercession. The point of these exercises is not to bring revelation from these images, but for these images to help bring revelation from the passage.

Many years ago, a lady gave a Pais director a copy of the famous black and white photo of construction workers sitting on a beam of an unfinished New York City skyscraper. Do you know the one I mean? In the picture, the men casually eat their packed lunches while sitting perched on an iron girder with their legs dangling high above the New York bustle.[65] She told my friend that this photo had spoken to her of the Pais leadership. They inspired her by living at such a height of faith, believing God for their provision, and yet seeming so relaxed. She said this gave her faith to believe God for her provision as well. I have used this photo to help people contemplate the parable of the talents:

> To those who use well what they are given, even more will be given, and they will have an abundance. [66]

I show the photo, remind them of the verse, and then pose the following question:

> What might God want of you that is a natural gift of yours but could be done to such a height of faith that it inspires others to use what God has given them?

Prompted by that, the Haverim contemplated the *personal* and *friendship* questions.

I have used video clips in this manner as well. Remember, the key is that the visual aid becomes no more than a catalyst to the passage of Scripture being contemplated.

Sound

We all know that music is a great aid to meditation. Besides blocking out other noises that can become a distraction, music inspires. Sometimes God uses music where teaching has failed. How many times have you seen someone caught up in worship to such an extent that they make a commitment to something they would not normally, rationally do? Why do so many men use background music to make their move and offer a proposal of marriage?

The Holy Spirit also uses sounds and melodies to pull our hearts in a direction that our minds stubbornly refuse to go.

A key to using music at the *inspired* level is to play something that does not have words. Instead, it should be chosen for its mood or emotional qualities—it may be stirring, it may be sad, it may be robust, it may be gentle. If you play a worship song, then the likelihood is that people's hearts and minds won't be tuned into the Holy Spirit, but tuned into the words of its composer.

Taste

Perhaps even the type of meal eaten when your Haverim gathers can spark revelation in the hearts of your group. God has used this sense many times throughout history, putting into place certain meals and feasts. He has led His people to specific types of food not to simply remind them of what has happened, but to connect them to a deeper level of the story. At times in Israel, people literally tasted their *Torah*.

Perhaps a creative Haverim host can participate in this level by occasionally prescribing a meal that acts as a stimulus to the study.

Smell

History tells us that the Church often used incense and smells to send a message. When Jesus appeared before Pilate, His body had been infused with expensive perfumes used for burials. He literally smelt of His death to come. When He stood before king and governor, although He said little with His lips, His body revealed through fragrance that His trials were a farce. What must God have revealed to His accusers simply by the smell of Jesus?

Just like music, we've all experienced how a sudden smell has taken us back to another time and place. Perhaps this sense can be creatively engaged at this level of our study.

Speech

I often find it helpful to keep a meditation exercise flowing by occasionally speaking simple words and phrases into the mix. As people are meditating on God and how He interacts with us, one idea is to occasionally throw into the mix one of the names of God. Invoking 'Jehovah,' 'Abba,' 'El Shaddai,'

'Elohim,' and other such descriptions not only provide food for thought, but also a catalyst for meditation. Long silences are sometimes best punctuated with words that keep people on track.

Touch

Objects don't have to be seen to help us believe. In one Haverim group a few months ago, an object was passed around veiled by a thin piece of cloth. The friends had to guess its identity. They then reflected on what it felt like to hold a truth in your hands but see it *dimly* through a veil.

Even touch can be used as a catalyst if the right questions are posed by the Haverim teacher.

Einstein

Questions, creativity, and community: all vital ingredients in the pursuit of Godly wisdom.

It would be a mistake to think that this fourth level of Haverim Devotions is a departure from rational thought. Even Einstein conducted what he called 'thought experiments.' I would have expected him to commit himself fully to research and calculations, and then deduce his theories. Instead, he day-dreamed. Occasionally he would be inspired, and then he researched to see if his revelation was correct. This was how he came up with the theories of general relativity and special relativity—by looking out his window or imagining a man falling off a roof in an elevator.

He had a revelation and then tested it to see if was true.

In a similar way, the process of the *inspired* level is that we pass on an impression that came to us while reflecting on Scripture and then find out through further study or communal feedback if our impression was indeed an inspiration from God.

One Pais director pointed out that it may be better on occasion to put *s'od* first in our study of a passage. Because the *inspired* level is last, it is some-times weakened due the fact that our minds are no longer virgin territory and have now been filled with the thoughts and ideas of everyone's interpretations. So, on occasion, moving the levels around may not only be productive, but may also free us from a regimented approach to Haverim Devotions.

However, remember that Einstein needed to know the basics of science first—the *p'shat*, if you like. Therefore, while the *inspired* level could come first, it is always important that at some point, we check our ideas with the filter of the *intended* level.

With that in mind, let me encourage you with one final observation:

> God is to be experienced!

He longs for us to search for Him in order to taste and see that He is good.

He does not simply want to be read about by students . . . He wants to be followed by disciples. God wants us to be those who practice His presence on a regular basis because we want to know Him, not simply know about Him.

Or, as one rabbi said:

> ". . . we walk around in pursuit of *p'shat* and afraid of *s'od*, thinking that we know all we must to make life work as it should, and then wonder why it doesn't. It is *s'od* that is closest to G-d in the hierarchy of learning, and though you can't soar in the clouds until you learn to first walk on earth, you must learn to walk on the earth with the goal to one day soar in the clouds."[67]

To do this we must stop *trying* and start *training*.

Summary

So let me summarize a suggested process for revealing *s'od*.

This level provides space for contemplation to discover how we can put what was learned into practice. Optionally, choose a creative catalyst to inspire thoughts about the passage that was studied. Prepare the atmosphere in advance in order to engage the senses through sight, smell, sound, touch, or taste. Ask the group to quietly contemplate the passage based on the following *personal* and *friendship* questions. After an allotted amount of time, use the *action point* to encourage the group to practice passing on revelation.

Optional Catalyst:

Use a creative tool to help people focus their contemplation.

Personal Questions:

Lord, what do I not yet understand about this passage?
What has previously been hidden to me?
What do You want me to do in response to this passage?

Friendship Questions:

Is there someone to whom I can pass on a message from this passage and how should I do that?

Action Point:

Share what God said to you and what He inspired you to tell others.

INFRASTRUCTURE

Practice makes permanent.

How?

Preparation

Essentially, there are two ways to facilitate a Haverim Bible study.

The first method is group-led where the Haverim members decide what and how to study. The second is facilitator-led whereby the leader determines how to proceed.

For this example, we will look at the facilitator-led method.

I have decided to use a familiar passage with few surprises; this is because my main aim is to show you how to take people through a devotion, not provide new insights into the passage. It is the one we looked at earlier in the 'What?' chapter of the *intended* level. In fact, you will want to quickly reread that section titled 'Context' to refresh your memory.

> *Now there was a Pharisee, a man named Nicodemus who was a member of the Jewish ruling council. He came to Jesus at night and said, "Rabbi, we know that you are a teacher who has come from God. For no one could perform the signs you are doing if God were not with him." Jesus replied, "Very truly I tell you, no one can see the kingdom of God unless they are born again." "How can someone be born when they are old?" Nicodemus asked. "Surely they cannot enter a second time into their mother's womb to be born!" Jesus answered, "Very truly I tell you, no one can enter the kingdom of God unless they are born of water and the Spirit."[68]*

Here are the three things you may want to do in advance:

1. Decide what it is you would like to discover and disclose.

It is important to note that you can enter Haverim Devotions with no idea where you are headed and do little preparation in advance. That can work fine. In fact, that may be necessary if you are in a one-to-one situation where you are helping someone with a specific question and are responding on the spot. However, in most cases, a little preparation can add a lot more power and purpose to a group study. When rabbis taught, they had the end in mind. Their aim was to facilitate a disciple's exploration of a subject, but they also had specific truths that they wanted to teach them. In the same way, we are hoping that our Haverim will discover all manner of treasures, but we may also want to ensure that they grasp a particular principle or theme.

In our chosen passage, I am hoping they will discover that Jesus was emphasizing a physical ceremony cannot save you, but a spiritual transformation needs to take place.

2. Decide which questions are relevant and which are not.

As I go through this study with you, notice that I have ignored some of the standard questions and I use only those that are particularly relevant. Remember, 'every Scripture has seventy facets' and therefore when you approach a passage, you do not need to uncover absolutely everything that is in it. So some of the standard questions will be more useful than others.

It is also important to note at this point that not all levels will yield balanced results. In other words, some passages will pack a bigger punch when you look at their context (*p'shat*) rather than their connections with other Scriptures (*r'mez*). Others may lend themselves to a particularly powerful collaborative exercise (*d'rash*), while some may be more dynamic when contemplating the Scripture and asking for revelation (*s'od*).

Do not to stress yourself out, as some leaders do, in trying to find a passage that is equally 'mind-blowing' at every level. Again, it is important to note, Haverim is as much about teaching us *how* to study any passage, as what we discover in any particular session.

For precept must be upon precept, precept upon precept; line upon line, line upon line; here a little, and there a little.[69]

So choose the questions that apply to your main point and allow study upon study to build holistically.

3. Decide if there are specific resources you want people to use.

Most of the time, the information required can be found in the general books and resources that we have already discussed. However, in some cases, you may realize that the information you especially want them to discover is in a certain book or on a particular blog or website. In those situations, you may need to provide the key sources.

Process

With that in mind, let me show you how I might lead a Haverim through John 3:1-5 using the four levels.

Intended Meaning | P'shat

At this level, we seek *context* to discover the main *point* by asking the *specific* and *generic* questions that follow. I have crossed out those that do not apply to our text.

Specific Question:

The *specific* question comes from what seems odd in the passage that might be better understood with an increased knowledge of its context. Therefore, I would ask:

In those days, were there other ways that someone might consider themselves 'born again'?

Generic Questions:

Who wrote it?

Why did they write it?

~~Where were they when they wrote it?~~

How is it affected by the manners and customs of the day?

~~What can archaeology teach us about this passage?~~

What does history teach us about the subject?

What happened to the main character(s) before or after the incident?

We would then look at the usual resources to find our answers. Because I am hoping my Haverim will discover the various ways the term 'born again' was used in Jesus's day, I would also provide a book or website that best summarizes the six ceremonies. Alternatively, I might post that section of the book on a blog and offer it as one of the online resources.

Action Point:

I would then ask my Haverim to share with each other what the context taught them about the main point of the passage.

Implied Meaning | R'mez

At the *implied* level, we seek *connections* to discover a *principle*. Therefore, I would ask the following *specific* and *generic* questions.

Specific Question:

Is there a pattern to be discovered or a principle to be applied?

Generic Questions:

Does the passage refer to another Scripture, story, or prophecy in the Bible?

Does anything referenced here have a meaning elsewhere in Scripture? (I might also add: For instance, where else in Scripture is the phrase 'born again' mentioned?)

My Haverim will likely find that there are two other incidents with Nicodemus in the book of John. Before the Pharisees in John 7:50-51, he defends Jesus and those who believe in Him. I would therefore expect them to realize that at some point, Nicodemus became either a follower of Jesus or at the very least a believer in Him.

Nowhere else in Scripture is Jesus recorded telling someone they must be born again and I am hoping my friends will understand Christ was making His message very specific to Nicodemus. However, in 1 Peter 1:23, the term is mentioned once more and emphasizes the differences between a perishable seed and an imperishable one. I am expecting that through this connection, they will see a principle developing: Nicodemus was a man whose connection to God was trusting in laws, ceremonies, and his ancestry as 'Abraham's seed,' but Jesus was saying that the connection the Father requires is based on a spiritual rebirth, not the traditions of man.

One of the facts that I hope will have been discovered from answering the *generic* questions is that in John 19:39-42, Nicodemus helped take care of Jesus's body and, importantly, the Bible highlights the fact that he understood and abided by the religious laws and ceremonies.

Therefore, one of the patterns that might be noticed is that Nicodemus was a man who held tightly to tradition, ceremony, and commandments, yet failed to see what he really needed to understand. From that, the group might find various principles in answer to the *specific* question, such as, laws help us know where we are failing, but rarely have the power to help us succeed.

Action Point:

I would then ask my Haverim to put their principles into a sound bite, diagram, or story in order to share it with others.

After they give theirs, I would give mine.

Interpreted Meaning | D'rash

At this *interpreted* level, we seek *collaboration* to discover the *purpose*. Here are the *specific* and *generic* instructions I would use to do that.

Specific Instructions:

Choose the character and verse(s) to interpret and ask why they did what they did.

Here, as usual, I have a choice. Do I use *d'rash* for the purpose of theology or anthropology—a study of God or a study of man? In other words, do I put my Haverim in the place of Jesus or Nicodemus? The principle I am promoting suggests that I choose the former. Among the other things they discover, I want them to understand the heart of God and what He is looking for in our relationship with Him. For that same reason, I would choose to *d'rash* John 3:2-3.

He came to Jesus at night and said, "Rabbi, we know that you are a teacher who has come from God. For no one could perform the signs you are doing if God were not with him." Jesus replied, "Very truly I tell you, no one can see the kingdom of God unless they are born again."

The specific question should be one that helps us discover the motive and the character's purpose. With that in mind regarding this particular passage, I would frame the question to be:

Why did Jesus choose this particular metaphor of being 'born again' rather than just telling Nicodemus straight what he needed to do?

I would then ask them to rewrite the verse in one to three sentences from Jesus's perspective, following the *generic* instructions.

Generic Instructions:

Rewrite the verse(s) in first person.
Include what the character may have been thinking or feeling.
Retell the story, fill in the gaps, but whatever you do, don't change the facts.

After allowing 5-10 minutes for them to *d'rash* the verses, I would introduce the *action point*.

Action Point:

Read out your *d'rash* and optionally use a creative tool to explain what you discovered.

To include a creative aspect, I might ask my Haverim to share their principle by creating a newspaper headline—something that shouts from the rooftops what was whispered in Nicodemus's ear at night.

After they share their *d'rash*, I would share mine:

Nicodemus approached me at night with his confession: "We know you are a teacher from God..." He sought truth but was limited by his trust in tradition. I needed to strip him of what he thought he knew in order to teach him what he needed to know. So I used a phrase that highlighted ceremonies he could never fulfill, saying, "Very truly I tell you, no one can see the kingdom of God unless they are born again."

My headline might be:

"Jesus strips Nicodemus of what he knows to help him see something new!"

One thing to note as a leader or facilitator is that, if you are concerned people may miss the main principle you want to teach, you can always include it in your own *d'rash*. For me, the truth discovered in this passage would help both Christians and non-Christians realize that we often need to put away our preconceived ideas before God can give us a better understanding of who He is.

Inspired Meaning | S'od

Finally, I would take my Haverim through *s'od*, which again may be on a different occasion from the other levels. Remember at this *inspired* level, we seek *contemplation* to discover a *practice*.

Nicodemus came at night and in those days, nighttime was not as artificially lit as it is today. It would have really been dark and so I want to add that to the mix. To me, this emphasizes the fact that Jesus is highlighting an unseen transformation, as opposed to ceremonies that are purposely visible. If I wanted to include an optional catalyst to help people focus their contemplation, I could do the following:

Optional Catalyst:

I might turn off all lights or cover any sunlight and ask my Haverim to contemplate this as a metaphor while they silently ask the following *personal* and *friendship* questions.

Personal Questions:

Lord, what do I not yet understand about this passage?
What has previously been hidden to me?
What do You want me to do in response to this passage?

Friendship Questions:

Is there someone to whom I can pass on a message from this passage and how should I do that?

After the group has been given time and space to contemplate, I would encourage the following *action point* with the caveat to share only if it will not embarrass anyone.

Action Point:

Share what God said to you and what He inspired you to tell others.

There is no way of knowing what will come out of this level but, as usual, I am hoping for some practical application of the passage and the principle they have learned. It could be that some people feel they need to engage with God's Holy Spirit more on a relational basis. Or perhaps someone will sense that a friend they know is bound up with legalization and needs prayer to understand more of God's grace.

What I will be confident of is that much of the revelation will be in line with the Word of God.

In doing all this, I would have helped them know *how* to study, not simply told them *what* to study. You can do this also. Once you study this way a few times, it will become second nature to you.

Practice rarely makes perfect, but often makes permanent!

Non-Stories

So, what if your passage is not a story?

What if it is a selection of one of Paul's epistles or a psalm of David?

Here are suggestions from my personal standpoint and those of my friends.

The *intended*, *implied*, and *inspired* levels are not really affected by the type of passage you are studying. However, when it gets to the *interpreted* level where the use of *d'rash* is required, some get confused. Occasionally I have been asked:

> How do you put yourself in the place of a character if there is no story with a character in it?

The answers are fairly simple.

First, you can put yourself in the place of the author of the letter, prophecy, psalm, etc. One of my wife's favorite books is *All the Men of the Bible*.[70] She loves it for this very reason; it helps her understand a little more the situation the writer of the passage was in and gives her insight into why they wrote it.

Secondly, writing a *d'rash* as one of the hearers of the passage might be an insightful experience. If you lived in Corinth, what might your reaction be when you heard the letter read out?

Thirdly, perhaps most helpfully, you can imagine yourself in the place of the Holy Spirit. Why did He inspire Paul to write what He wrote to Timothy in a particular verse? Or even more intriguing, what do you think the Father feels when He hears David's poem sung by His people?

But what about subject or topic-based studies?

What if you are approaching the Bible from the perspective of finding strength in difficult times, conquering temptation, or winning others to the faith? Of course you can still apply the methods I have previously mentioned, but there is tip I would like to share with you . . .

In the Pais Movement, we train our apprentices who work in schools to prepare any teaching they create in the following manner. After receiving a topic from a teacher and before they start to create a lesson plan, we ask them to 'haverim' the subject. (Yes, we even use it as a verb now!) For instance, let's say that the school asks them to support the staff in an anti-bullying campaign and the subject on which they are asked to prepare material is peer-pressure. In this case, before they brainstorm ideas or rush to include a cool video or skit they once saw, we ask them to find their core message and points by taking the subject through the four levels of Haverim Devotions.

To do this, they first choose a Bible study that contains peer pressure within it. For example, they might choose the story of Eve's temptation of Adam or Peter's denial of Christ to the servant girl. They may also want to find a verse that they can use as an anchor point—something like 1 Corinthians 10:13:

> No temptation has overtaken you except what is common to mankind. And God is faithful; he will not let you be tempted beyond what you can bear. But when you are tempted, he will also provide a way out so that you can endure it.

By doing this, they will gather the core of a message for the students, plus the conviction they need by placing themselves within the message and feeling what needs to be felt. When they teach, depending on the laws of the nation they are in, they may or may not actually use that Scripture. If they are not allowed to introduce the Bible, they may still make up a parallel analogy since young people grasp a message better if it is contained within a story narrative.

So how does that help us?

Well, if we want to take our Haverim through the study of a subject, we can do the same; we can either look at a passage that contains that subject and/or pick a story from the Bible that includes it. However, it is key that the purpose remains spiritual transformation, not simple behavior modification.

Haverim is designed to be versatile. You will get to experience this the more you grasp its principles.

Individuals

Can you use the four levels of Haverim Devotions on your own?

Absolutely!

For a start, it is a great way of training yourself for when you lead a Haverim. The Pais Global resource team, which my wife is part of, goes through a Haverim study on Tuesday to Friday mornings. On the Monday, the chosen facilitator for that week prepares the study by first going through the passage. This is when they choose a principle or theme they wish to highlight, decide which of the questions to use, plus any extra resources they wish to provide.

Also, as a general study tool for you as an individual, Haverim is great. You may not get the direct advantage of other people's *d'rash*, but all the levels are still very beneficial. In fact, I spent a couple of years going through various books of the Bible on my own using the four levels and suddenly realized that I had written commentaries on several books of the Bible without initially intending to. So I now have a great pool of background, context, insights, and principles which I can draw from when I preach or teach.

Lastly, training yourself consistently in Haverim Devotions means you will have a far greater capacity to help others discover God in the moments when you do not have time to prepare.

You see, there is a paradox within learning—the better you know how something works, the more freedom you will find to be creative without compromising the principles that make it work.

Haverim is to be your servant. You should not become its slave.

Who?

Everyone

Everyone.

That is who Haverim is for.

It is inclusive rather than exclusive in a way that no other Bible study method I know has been. Today the Oxford Dictionary announced that their Word of the Year is 'post-truth,'[71] an adjective defined as:

> Relating to or denoting circumstances in which objective facts are less influential in shaping public opinion than appeals to emotion and personal belief.

The upshot is that 'experts' who provide facts are less respected than they perhaps should be. Instead, communal learning where personal thoughts, feelings, and experiences are shared dominate the higher moral ground. This in many ways is troubling . . . unless we embrace the possibilities.

The reality is that Haverim is able to bring truth seamlessly into this post-truth world.

In his blog, "How can the Church survive our post-truth society?" one European pastor explains:

> ". . . I do think we need to be studying the Scriptures collaboratively. It's why I love the Haverim groups run by Pais. Haverim is a method of learning the truths of Christianity in which most members of the

group are active participants in the forming of the message. At the Haverim group I attended for eight weeks, experts were involved, but mainly via smartphone web searches. People discovered the knowledge for themselves via the Internet and shared those discoveries in the group. This is a teaching method that sits well in Adam Curtis's post-truth world—everyone is given credence and the expert in the room doesn't dominate the discussion."[72]

In my book, *Talmidim: How to Disciple Anyone in Anything*, I teach the dynamics of moving from 'one-to-many' to 'many-to-many'; in other words, how to activate a group that teaches itself rather than have one expert teach everyone. The benefit of this approach is that it opens up the possibility of a far broader audience or group of participants because not everyone has to be a follower of one particular leader. They just have to be seekers of truth.

In a Haverim, the role of the teacher is to facilitate the *'pull'* rather than present the *'push.'* To lead and occasionally fill in the gaps. With this in mind, the four levels of the Haverim Devotions become something you can also do with someone of no faith, little faith, or even another faith.

It is a 'one-space-fits-all' idea.

Non-Christians

So how do those not following Jesus respond to the four levels?

Here are some thoughts based on feedback from those who have been on the journey so far.

Intended | P'shat

Perhaps most surprising is the positive reaction to the *intended* meaning, the *p'shat*.

Non-Christians get to see the historical context that lies behind what we are studying. In doing so, they begin to realize that the Bible isn't just a bunch of stories hanging in a vacuum of fantasy. When people see archaeology, history, and literature outside of the Bible connecting with the stories, prophecies, and history within it, credibility is given to its content.

Depending on your group, you may want to encourage people to bring any research books they wish to this level of study, such as material explaining the history, customs, or practices of the period into which you are looking. They do not have to be the kind of book you find in a religious store. If it is not seen as a Christian book, yet provides context and couples well with the Bible passage, then perhaps this is even more powerful! Again, it raises a person's awareness of the Bible as an authentic historical document.

Implied | R'mez

For *r'mez*, they experience the fluidity of the Scriptures and how things correlate. Specifically, they get to see how the Messianic psalms and prophecies work together and how Scripture helps interpret itself and future things. For instance, when they research the context of Psalm 22 and study the facts to realize how long it was written before Jesus's declaration in Matthew 27 . . . they receive the same kind of goosebump effect I did.

For both the *intended* and *implied* levels, consider how you can help those who may be less literate than yourself. The level of academia can be simply determined by the kind of material you give them to research. For instance, I recently advised a Pais team working with a group of young people with low education not to give out books to use for research purposes, but instead create a fact sheet. I suggested it could be a mixture of simple information in both word and picture format—a sheet that is already compiled by the leaders and relates to the particular topic they are studying.

Love finds a way.

Interpreted | D'rash

D'rash goes down great with those not yet following Christ because people like to tell their own story. They like to express themselves in a particular situation that has already happened, and it helps them to discover and chat through their own motives. *D'rash* helps people relate to a book which they never thought they could!

Ultimately, our friends can come to terms with why the characters in the stories did what they did—even if that character is or represents God. They begin to associate and feel for the Scripture they are reading as they become emotionally, not just mentally, involved.

Inspired | S'od

S'od is an interesting one with non-believers.

How can the Spirit speak to those He does not live within?

You might be surprised. The impact of someone praying for you is, as someone mentioned last night in the Haverim on our street, "a bonding experience."

Coming into a safe environment to be quiet, reflect, and meditate while others do the work can be very enticing to some, especially if they suddenly feel connected to the people of God in a way they may never have felt before.

You may be reading this thinking, 'I just can't see it.'

Well, if you are imagining strangers, you would be right. Remember, a Haverim is a group of friends who study together. Imagine, therefore, those of no faith, little faith, or another faith wanting to explore faith. Think of people with whom you have made authentic friendships.

With such people, Haverim works.

Just let me reiterate, in case you are confused. Haverim has two parts: the Haverim and Haverim Devotions.

A Haverim is a group whose primary intention is to know God and make Him known. Haverim Devotions is the tool, the method of study by which to explore the God of the Bible. This method is used within the Haverim, but can also be used separately from it. My prayer is that Haverim Devotions or any part of them never become a gimmick or a fun way to add a bit of spice to a traditional Bible study.

The motive behind the method is mission.

You can use just one level of Haverim Devotions in a lunchtime conversation where you simply get someone to *d'rash* a story. The story could be a passage about the thing they are going through, perhaps a parable. The story might not even be a Biblical one. Instead, it may be a story you made up that contains a truth about the Kingdom, or you could give them a Biblical story set in a modern day era.

You can use it anywhere as my friend Wayne once did on a plane. Here is his experience in his own words:

> "Sitting next to a stranger on a flight, I felt prompted to engage him in a conversation. I am the first to admit that I have a difficult time talking to strangers, particularly about spiritual matters. However, in our Haverim we had been thinking through how to find the *interpreted* meaning, and it opened my eyes to an easy and natural opportunity. So I leaned over and said, 'I'm tackling a question about the Bible here. It deals with the story of Noah and the flood. It asks why would a loving God wipe out most of the human race. I wonder if you can help me?' He said he was happy to discuss the topic and so, within the context of a casual conversation, he and I *d'rashed* a key verse in the story. Together we looked at sin through God's perspective."

Putting oneself in place of someone in authority is something we do all the time. "If I were the president, I would..." So, because the *interpreted* level basically asks you to do that from God's point-of-view, Wayne didn't feel out of his comfort zone to ask a perfect stranger that question. It was a question that then opened the door to a genuine conversation about God's heart.

Just another example of how Haverim allows you to study anything with anyone . . . and at any time!

Frequency

As long as Haverim is used to train the Church to reach out, then I have no desire to promote a particular way of using it. Again, let Haverim Devotions be your servant; do not become a slave to a particular system. If you look for #haverimdevotions on social media, you may find new ideas from others.

I do, however, have suggestions for those asking the question, 'How many levels should I attempt in one session?'

The One-Session Study

When studying in a small group, home group, or worship service, then all four levels of Haverim Devotions can be attempted in one session. However, I would suggest that the first two levels are tackled simultaneously and your group is split into smaller groups for those sections.

Recently, after presenting a master class on Haverim, I was invited to lead a worship service using the method.[73] Occasionally, I find it helpful to concentrate on two or three levels in one session, and in this case, I skipped the *implied* level. The advantage of this is to focus on the levels that might be most productive for a particular passage of Scripture while avoiding the pressure of fitting everything into a short time frame.

> Pros: You can get through a lot of Scriptures and therefore learn the study method quickly.

> Cons: You may have little time for anything else, such as sharing a meal together or prayer.

The Two-Session Study

This perhaps provides the greatest balance between study and the other aspects of a group. The first week, the *intended* and *implied* levels of study are examined. Both levels naturally fit together because they are research-based. The second week, the *interpreted* and *inspired* levels are explored as they are both creativity-based.

Pros: You can cover a lot of ground but still have time for people to share their thoughts and feelings.

Cons: As with any compromise, you cannot please all the people all of the time.

The Three-Session Study

This is the most you will want to give to one passage of Scripture. You would examine the first two levels on one week and then the other two levels on separate weeks.

Pros: You can go into real depth and everyone can have extended time to share their discoveries.

Cons: You will cover far less Scripture over an extended period of time and people might get bored.

In the past, my Haverim operated a three-week strategy and met for two hours. The first half hour we ate, the next hour we studied, and the final half hour we relaxed together. The fourth week was when we outreached in order to make friends with the community. However, in the new Haverim I just planted in my community, we are going to a two-week strategy as I believe this will provide a greater balance. Plus, it means we can more rapidly respond to the topics that our friends want to study.

Of course there is no rule to say that you have to include all four levels every time you look at a passage. If you only have time to employ two or three levels, that's fine! Just mix it up a little so that over time, you and your Haverim, are familiar with all four levels and feel confident enough to use them with nonbelievers.

Friends

Haverim works because it is made up of friends who study together.

It must be stressed, however, that a major purpose of Haverim is to reach out to those who do not yet know Christ. This means not simply relying on old friends to attend, but proactively seeking to make new friends in our community.

In my previous Haverim, we did three-session studies, and on the fourth week, we reached out to our neighbors. Before I explain how we did that, let me introduce you to a couple of my friends and let you hear their story.

Over the past few years, it has been my pleasure to get to know Jonny and Vanessa, a young married couple who eagerly desire to share with their neighbors the faith they are excited about. Both are heavily involved in their local church activities, yet uncommonly, they still make time to touch the lives of those not a part of a church. Jonny works in his local Starbucks as a barista, and every one of his colleagues has visited his Haverim. Several are now part of it. Their Haverim has a mixture of ethnicity, so house parties with a different cultural theme such as Hispanic or German work great for every fourth week. They have held African, English, and Asian parties with food and games from those regions.

Here is their experience with Haverim in their own words:

> "Vanessa and I started out with parties. We love to throw parties. Ever since we arrived in St. Louis, we have hosted parties for friends to come and hang out and meet other people. This spectrum of people is quite broad—people we met that day all the way to our very own families. It doesn't matter what faith or background you have, it's all about coming and being served good food and drink and getting to know people of a beautiful culture and ethnicity.

> "This has really provided opportunities for us to begin a conversation with our community about the journey of faith we are all on. Haverim Devotions helps us do this as it opens up deep conversations. People can bring their journeys and experiences to the table without having to push them through a Christian filter. Pain, frustration, confusion about who God is—these are things we all experience, and this brings us together as people on the journey of faith.

"Haverim Devotions provides a tool that Christians, atheists, agnostics, Muslims, Jews, and every other religion and worldview can use to express their ideas and go deeper into learning who the one true God is. To us, it really has been about becoming a family. No matter what differences of opinion we have or what different faiths we have, we love each other and see one another as our very own.

"We also serve together. One day of every month, we seek to fulfill our community's biggest need. So Haverim to me is a place of peace, friendship, love, and faith all lived out as a family together."

I love their story. Mine is a bit different.

Texas lends itself to cookouts, and so our Haverim put the grill on the front driveway and invited the neighbors. We had face-painting for the children and a Slip 'N Slide. We put out chairs and invited neighbors to chat and play lawn games. We passed out flyers to the connecting streets each month, but we did not give a label to our group. We just announced them as neighborhood parties or events. I'm thinking of changing that in the future.

These simple activities earned very positive comments from our neighbors. A typical statement I heard was: "We have often said our community needs something like this, but we never knew how to start it or what to do."

We have since moved from our old home, but last time I spoke with one of my neighbors, he and his wife had started attending church.

Apart from community *recreational* events, the fourth week can also provide an opportunity for community *service* projects where the Haverim offers practical support to an individual or partners with a neighborhood project. This again provides an opportunity for the Haverim to be a catalyst in the community, offering a chance for those people of peace who are service-oriented in their personality to get involved and journey with you.

Haverim, you see, can be a tool for both mission and discipleship.

Organize

Again, the way you set up the leadership of your home-based Haverim is up to you. We split it into three roles rather than put all the responsibility on one person or couple, which has proven difficult for other small group formats. The three duties are as follows:

The Haverim *host* houses the Haverim if it meets in a home. They offer their hospitality and coordinate the food. They tidy the house and set it up for the meeting.

The Haverim *leader* is responsible for overseeing the group. They determine the recreational events and organize the people. They oversee the logistics and encourage us to keep on track with the vision.

The Haverim *teacher* is responsible for the studies. They determine the passages of Scripture with the group and lead many of the studies, but also train others within the group to teach as well.

A typical Haverim meeting does need some coordination, and having appointed leaders helps.

Another choice you have is what subjects to look at.

A Haverim can be used in two ways. One way is to unpack the material that the church is currently teaching; alternatively, the subject matter can be determined by those in the group. The first will give more ownership of the church's teaching and the second will allow the Haverim the flexibility it may require to reach out and engage others in their community.

Can I suggest you mix it up a little and use both?

In my book *Shalom: How to Reach Anyone Anywhere*,[74] I explain that the different approach Pais uses was one of the dynamics that helped get our teams into schools that had previously rejected other organizations. We never offered a pre-programmed package, carefully manicured with a bow on it. Instead, we offered role models who could prepare a presentation on anything the school wanted as long as it was based on common values.

This is also a benefit of Haverim and Haverim Devotions. The study can be done in response to the needs of those attending rather than deciding in advance what we think they might want or need to hear. This in itself can make Haverim very attractive.

The group may want to look at a certain difficult subject, a question of theology they have often struggled with, or a fascinating story. Your neighbors, however, may wish to tackle something topical that has raised issues in their lives. They know you are a Christian and now, facing a particular situation, they may need someone to help them navigate and understand what they are going through.

You must be flexible.

Will those who *don't* profess Christ as their savior really want to engage in the Word of God?

Yes . . . if they are given space to share their own thoughts.

Yes . . . if they are given the Spirit as their primary teacher.

Yes . . . if they are given the right to be wrong . . . and the right to be right.

Children

Churches worldwide are using Haverim and adapting it with different audiences. Many of the questions I get are from those looking to use it in a specific community or with a specific demographic, such as children.

Obviously young ones may struggle with some of the more complex principles and connections in a passage plus the resources adults might use for research. We want to pass on the principles of Haverim with practices that are similar but may not perfectly match what we do with adults. With that in mind, we can still teach them how they can *pull* information rather than waiting for someone to give it them.

The following are some very simple ideas to use as a launch pad.

Intended | P'shat

In the *intended* level for smaller children, we can use fact sheets with the contextual information they need to find already on it. You then turn it into a game, explaining that on the worksheet there are six different facts, three which are helpful to understand the story better and three which are not. With their friends, they can figure out which three are relevant and why.

This will do a number of things. First, it shows them that external resources help us understand the Bible more. Second, it teaches them how to *pull* out what is helpful and what is not. Third, they will learn how to study with their friends.

Implied | R'mez

In the *implied* level you can do something similar by putting potentially connected Scriptures on a worksheet. Sesame Street, the classic American children's program, had a song with the lines, "One of these things is not like the others. One of these things doesn't belong. Can you tell which thing is not like the others by the time I finish this song?"

Maybe we can reverse that by asking them which verses go together . . . and why?

Children can grasp principles if you teach them how to.

Interpreted | D'rash

As it stands, the *interpreted* level is no problem for children. They love to share their ideas and it only takes a couple of times for them to grasp the concept of *d'rash*.

Inspired | S'od

The *inspired* level is an interesting one when it relates to children depending on your particular doctrinal stance on the Holy Spirit. Some of you may want to use this level to help them simply reflect on the passage and share their thoughts. For others, you might see this as an opportunity to start training children to hear the Holy Spirit. I will leave the specifics to you, but I think most of us agree that God can speak directly to the little ones that God puts in our care.

> *The boy Samuel ministered before the Lord under Eli . . . Then the Lord called Samuel. Samuel answered, "Here I am." And he ran to Eli and said, "Here I am; you called me." But Eli said, "I did not call; go back and lie down."* [75]

This happened a second and then a third time . . .

> *A third time the Lord called, "Samuel!" And Samuel got up and went to Eli and said, "Here I am; you called me." Then Eli realized that the Lord was calling the boy. So Eli told Samuel, "Go and lie down, and if he calls you, say, 'Speak, Lord, for your servant is listening.'" So Samuel went and lay down in his place. The Lord came and stood there, calling as at the other times, "Samuel! Samuel!" Then Samuel said, "Speak, for your servant is listening."* [76]

God is speaking to children more often than they realize.

Sadly, however, few of them have an Eli to show them how to listen.

The key for this level is that we want to train children to meditate and listen for God's voice. We also want to teach them how to discern and obey. It does not need to be an intense experience, we just need to create space and the right kind of boundaries.

Haverim works with everyone!

Any age, any ethnicity, any stage of leaning forward.

When?

Traffic

May I ask a question of those ministers who have taken the time out of their hectic schedules to read this book?

What is the role of Christian leadership?

What were we called by Jesus to do when we were appointed to lead God's people? To manage expectations? Or to help advance the Kingdom of God in the lives of those we lead and those they touch? So many ministers of Christ are so wrapped up in the former activity that we have perhaps come to doubt that our congregations would be able to make friends and communicate their faith in the way of Haverim. But, whose fault is that?

I don't think we can put the blame on our culture because our society is crying out for what we have experienced. We just need a different way to share it with them. Is it really that our people cannot reach their neighbors or that our *church* culture has not yet provided them the strategy and opportunity to do it in a way they know will work?

Maybe Jesus's brother was right . . .

> *You do not have, because you do not ask . . .*[77]

I know our congregations can do this if they are challenged to do it because I see it happening virally worldwide. Yet, I wonder how much more impactful they could become if we not only gave people permission but a plan?

I have lived in the city of Arlington, Texas, for several years now. It has well over 300,000 residents and lies in the middle of the metroplex, a conglomeration of many other cities including Dallas, Fort Worth, and, north of us, two of the fastest growing cities in America. It has two local airports; the largest is said to be bigger than Manhattan Island! Yet, since we emigrated from England, I have been in a major traffic jam only a handful of times. Some may say I just need to get out more . . . Possibly true, but I think there may be another reason.

Texas was built with the car in mind.

In England, our historic cities were established before the production of cars was a twinkle in Henry Ford's eye. Back home, the roads are narrow, winding, and squeeze themselves into the small spaces remaining after hundreds of years of industrial development. Yet in Texas, visionary genius lies behind the way its road systems were designed. Huge, wide-open highways were cut through the state before the need for many of them had arisen.

When it comes to *mission*, *discipleship*, and *study*, our sermons may reveal that these things are in our hearts, but do our programs and strategies betray the fact that they take a back seat to attraction and assimilation?

When will we all agree that we need large, attractive churches, but designed from the foundation up with an approach to the Word of God that can go viral? When will we commit to a study of the Scriptures that helps the saints understand the *heart* of God, not just His rules and rewards? When will we create, promote, and teach a form of Bible study that can be passed on by the average Christian to their neighbor? When will we even see that as important?

When will we redesign our programs to produce the kind of people who will participate in the mission Jesus had in mind?

When will we be able to truly believe in all that we do?

This very last question has haunted me for the past 25 years. It first led me to establish the Pais Project, now working in public schools on six continents. It has also encouraged us to create the Pais Collective, Pais Infrastructure, and Pais Venture in order to provide churches, non-profits, and businesses with a compelling response to a changing world in the areas of *mission*, *discipleship*, and *study*.

All three books I have written on these subjects are intended to pose questions, not pull down what went before. Instead, they seek to build on what we have achieved so far and suggest a way forward. Because I do see a way forward . . . and it excites me!

Velocity

The world is not changing; the world *has* changed.

At the end of the last century, in his book *Business @ the Speed of Thought*, Bill Gates declared that for successful business in the eighties, the key word had been 'quality,' in the nineties it was 'innovation,' and he prophesied that in the noughties, it would be 'velocity.'[78] He suggested that the companies that would do best in the new century would be those who could respond most quickly to the changing needs of its clients. I remember thinking to myself at the time how sad it is that the world responds so speedily to the 'holy customer' and yet the Church responds so slowly to the Holy Spirit.

The world has changed . . . It is *reverting*.

The ways in which Jesus understood and unpacked the Scriptures are in vogue. More than that, they are essential. To comprehend the Bible in a way that will open up a whole new world for us, we must grasp hold of what Jesus understood it to be. Then, we can let His *message* contained within it shape our *methods* for teaching it. To do this, He wishes to lead us through *experience*, giving us a method where we can *participate* in the study of God's heart. He wants to pose questions in our *imagination* in order that we can *connect* with one another no matter what our background, age, culture, or even . . . beliefs. Then, together, we can learn to help everyone study anything with everyone.

Or as the ancient Hebrews once referred to it . . . *Haverim*.

INFORMATION

#haverimdevotions

What?

Are you confused? Is this all too much? Are you unsure how the different levels fit together? Have you noted that each level has words beginning with the letters 'I', 'C', and 'P', as well as Hebrew words that are supposed to connect in some kind of way, but you are not sure how?

Let me suggest that you go to haverimdevotions.com where you can find more resources, such as a visual template and answers to frequently asked questions. Also, see 'Haverim Devotions: At a Glance' below. It allows you to take a step back and see how everything joins together.

Thanks again for reading the book. I really hope it helps you discover new truths and gives you the confidence needed to study God's heart with anyone.

Haverim Devotions: At a Glance

The following are my suggestions for implementing each level:

Intended | *P'shat* | Context to discover the Point

At this level, the group utilizes a variety of books, websites, and other study resources to examine the context of the passage in order to discover its intended point. Organize the Haverim into groups of twos and threes. Discuss the *specific* question and assign the *generic* questions to each group, ignoring those not applicable to the passage. After an allotted time for research, ask the groups to share their discoveries. Finally, use the *action point* to encourage each person to summarize the main point.

Specific Question:

What seems odd that might be better understood with an increased knowledge of its context?

Generic Questions:

Who wrote it?
Why did they write it?
Where were they when they wrote it?
How is it affected by the manners and customs of the day?
What can archaeology teach us about this passage?
What does history teach us about the subject?
What happened to the main character(s) before or after the incident?

Action Point:

Share what the context taught you about the main point of the passage.

Implied | *R'mez* | Connections to discover the Principle

Frequently combined with the *intended* level, this *implied* level also utilizes Bible study resources to find *connections* in Scripture that lead to a *principle*. Organize the Haverim into groups of twos and threes, providing each group with the following *specific* and *generic* questions. After an allotted time for research, ask the groups to share their discoveries with the rest of the Haverim. Use the *action point* to prompt each person to summarize a principle from the passage.

Specific Question:

Is there a pattern to be discovered or a principle to be applied?

Generic Questions:

Does the passage refer to another Scripture, story, or prophecy in the Bible? Does anything referenced here have a meaning elsewhere in Scripture?

Action Point:

Put this principle into a sound bite, diagram, or story to share.

Interpreted | *D'rash* | Collaboration to discover the Purpose

At this level, we insert ourselves into Scripture in order to reveal a motive. To determine which character and verse(s) to interpret (*d'rash*), decide if you want to gain perspective into the human heart or into God's heart. After choosing the character and verse(s), tailor your specific question to the passage by asking 'why'. For example, 'Why did Jehoash strike the ground only three times?' (Human perspective.) Or, 'Why did God instruct the angel to wrestle with Jacob?' (God's perspective.) Allow 5 to 10 minutes of silence to complete the *generic* instructions. Use the *action point* to encourage people to share their interpretations with the group. Allow time to collaborate on how these interpretations can be applied.

Specific Instructions:

Choose the character and verse(s) to interpret and ask why they did what they did.

Generic Instructions:

Rewrite the verse(s) in first person.
Include what the character may have been thinking or feeling.
Retell the story, fill in the gaps, but whatever you do, don't change the facts.

Action Point:

Read out your *d'rash* and optionally use a creative tool to explain what you discovered.

Inspired | S'od | Contemplation to discover the Practice

This level provides space for contemplation to discover how we can put what was learned into practice. Optionally, choose a creative catalyst to inspire thoughts about the passage that was studied. Prepare the atmosphere in advance in order to engage the senses through sight, smell, sound, touch, or taste. Ask the group to quietly contemplate the passage based on the following *personal* and *friendship* questions. After an allotted amount of time, use the *action point* to encourage the group to practice passing on revelation.

Optional Catalyst:

Use a creative tool to help people focus their contemplation.

Personal Questions:

Lord, what do I not yet understand about this passage?
What has previously been hidden to me?
What do You want me to do in response to this passage?

Friendship Questions:

Is there someone to whom I can pass on a message from this passage and how should I do that?

Action Point:

Share what God said to you and what He inspired you to tell others.

#haverimdevotions

JOIN THE DISCUSSION
haverimdevotions.com

Endnotes

1. Phoebe Hill, "Why the Church Doesn't Have to Lose a Generation of Young People," *Christian Today*, December 16, 2016. http://www.christiantoday.com/article/why.the. church.doesnt.have.to.lose.a.generation.of.young.people/103081.htm.

2. I am referencing Max Lucado, Bill Hybels, Rick Warren, and Francis Chan. They are all great writers whom I respect; therefore, this comment is not a reflection on them, but upon those of us who read them.

3. Hebrews 5:12.

4. Leonard Sweet, *Post-Modern Pilgrims: First Century Passion for the 21st Century World* (Nashville: Boardman & Holman Publishers, 2000).

5. Brian Stelter, "Youths Are Watching, but Less Often on TV." *New York Times Online*, February 8, 2012. http://www.nytimes.com/2012/02/09/business/media/young-people-are-watching-but-less-often-on-tv.html?pagewanted=all&_r=0.

6. Acts 8:30-31 NLT.

7. CNN (2011). *Interview with James Dyson.* Interviewed by Fareed Zakara [TV] November 27, 2011.

8. This time period was between 530 BC and 70 AD when the Second Temple of Jerusalem was in place and in which the Gospels and most of the book of Acts took place.

9. Haverim Devotions™ is trademarked by Paul Clayton Gibbs. To complement the teaching of this study method contained in this book, more information can be found at haverim-devotions.com.

10. David H. Stern, *Jewish New Testament Commentary* (Clarksville, MD: Jewish New Testament Publications, Inc., 1992), pg. 11-12.

11. Babylonian Talmud Hagigah 14b; Jerusalem Talmud Hagigah 2:1.

12. Matthew 13:3-23.

13. Many of the parables Jesus told were twists on those that already existed. The parable of the four soils was His contribution to an often-used rabbinic formula. The *mishnah*, which means 'repetition,' and is the collection of oral tradition of Jewish law, utilizes it in the parable of the four kitchen utensils: the sponge, the funnel, the strainer, and the sift. Gamaliel, a well-respected Jewish teacher and contemporary of Jesus, spoke of the parable of four fish: the fish that is unclean, the fish that is clean, the fish from the Jordan River, and the fish from the Mediterranean. Why were the parables of the four hearers so popular? Because they were the perfect formula to teach the commodity that leads to multiplication as shown in Matthew 13:23: *"But the seed falling on good soil refers to someone who hears the word and understands it. This is the one who produces a crop, yielding a hundred, sixty or thirty times what was sown."* That commodity is . . . understanding.

14. Matthew 13:4.

15. This is the more typical phrase that is used by rabbis based on scriptures such as Talmud Shabbat 63a when Rabbi Kahana objected to Mar son of Rabbi Huna: "A verse cannot depart from its plain meaning."

16. Torah is defined as "the body of wisdom and law contained in Jewish Scripture and other sacred literature and oral tradition" and "the five books of Moses constituting the Pentateuch." Merriam Webster, s.v. "Torah," accessed April 23, 2013, http://www.merriam-webster.com/dictionary/torah.

17. Dr. Ron Moseley, *Yeshua: A Guide to the Real Jesus and the Original Church* (Clarksville, MD: Messianic Jewish Publishers, 1996), pg. 126-7.

18. John 3:5.

19. John 11:17.

20. David H. Stern, *Jewish New Testament Commentary* (Clarksville, MD: Jewish New Testament Publications, Inc., 1992), pg. 189-190.

21. Jesus raised the widow's son at Nain in Luke 7:11-17 and Jairus's daughter in Matthew 9:18-26.

22. Acts 15:28-29.

23. The Noahide laws are recognized as traditional ethical values (*The Jewish New Testament Commentary*, 278). During the 102nd Congress of the United States of America, March 5, 1991, they were referenced as the ethical values and principles at the bedrock of society. *Tosefta* refers to the collection of traditions in the Jewish oral law (*Jewish Encyclopedia*, http://www.jewishencyclopedia.com/articles/14458-tosefta). *Talmud* here is a generic designation for an entire body of Jewish literature which includes writings of Jewish tradition (*Jewish Encyclopedia*, http://www.jewishencyclopedia.com/articles/14213-talmud).

24. In the past, I have used books such as Freeman's *Manners and Customs of the Bible*, *In Search of Paul* by John Dominic Crossan and Jonathan Reed, or *The Parables* by Brad Young.

25. Two I have used in the past are *Baker Encyclopedia of Christian Apologetics* and *Hard Sayings of the Bible*, but many others are available.

26. Brad Young, *The Parables: Jewish Tradition and Christian Interpretation* (Peabody, MA: Hendrickson Publishers, 1998).

27. Share your ideas on the website haverimdevotions.com where you can find pools of helpful suggestions and resources.

28. Matthew 13:5-6.

29. Matthew 27:46.

30. Psalm 22:14-18.

31. Psalm 22:23-24; 27; 29-31.

32. Matthew 11:3.

33. Matthew 11:4-5.

34. Matthew 11:6.

35. According to the Jews, this is implied in Isaiah 11:1-2, but not made specific. See note on Matthew 11:3-6 from the *Jewish New Testament Commentary*. David H. Stern, *Jewish New Testament Commentary* (Clarksville, MD: Jewish New Testament Publications, Inc., 1992).

36. Matthew 11:28-30.

37. Matthew 21:15-16.

38. Psalm 8:2 NIV 1984 ed.

39. Matthew 21:17.

40. Luke 22:42. Story also in Matthew 26.

41. Zechariah 14:4-5.

42. Matthew 26:31 quoting Zechariah 13:7.

43. Matthew 13:7.

44. Matthew 13:52.

45. All of the sages said this, but it is stated in Bamidbar Rabba 13:15, which is a Jewish document, a *d'rash* or *midrash* from classical Judaism.

46. David Bivin, *New Light on the Difficult Words of Jesus: Insights from His Jewish Context* (En-Gedi Resource Center, 2005), pg. 157.

47. 2 Kings 13:14-19.

48. 2 Kings 13:14b.

49. After studying context for a while, you will begin to store away all sorts of information that becomes applicable to many different Scriptures. This was the case here. Although I cannot remember exactly where I originally learned this tidbit; I believe it was from Jack Hayford, *The Hayford Bible Handbook* (Nashville: Thomas Nelson, Inc., 1995).

50. In Matthew 16:18, Peter is told he is on the attack, not the defense. Jesus spoke these words to Peter in Caesarea Philippi, a center of pagan worship that was believed to be an entrance to the underworld. Because gates represent defense, Jesus (obviously the Godly influence here) infers that Peter is on the attack, taking ground from Hell. Whereas some Christians may think that Hell is advancing, in actuality, the Kingdom of God is advancing and Hell cannot withstand it.

51. 2 Kings 13:18-19.

52. Matthew 14:22-27.

53. A study of God, not a study of people.

54. Genesis 32:24.

55. John 15:15.

56. Matthew 13:8.

57. Forrest Gump's mother in the movie *Forrest Gump*.

58. Galatians 1:11-16.

59. These are two Scriptures that attest to this: Colossians 2:2-3: (". . . *in order that they may know the mystery [s'od] of God, namely, Christ* [Messiah], *in whom is hidden all the treasures of wisdom & knowledge*") and 1 Corinthians 2:7 *(". . . we declare God's wisdom, a mystery [s'od] that has been hidden and that God destined for our glory before time began"*).

60. Numbers 11:25.

61. Numbers 11:29.

62. Luke 5:4-6.

63. This book is the third in the Kingdom Trilogy, which consists of *The Kingdom Pioneers* (Previously titled *The Line and the Dot*, 2010, 2014), *The Kingdom Principles* (Previously titled *The Cloud and the Line*, 2011), and *The Kingdom Patterns* (Previously titled *The Seed and the Cloud*, 2016).

64. Matthew 6:33.

65. To view the photo I'm describing, 'Lunch atop a Skyscraper (New York Construction Workers Lunching on a Crossbeam),' go to http://en.wikipedia.org/wiki/Lunch_atop_a_Skyscraper.

66. Matthew 25:29 NLT.

67. Rabbi Pinchas Winston. "Just Desserts," Torah.org, 1995-2007, http://www.torah.org/learning/perceptions/5761/bamidbar.html.

68. John 3:1-5.

69. Isaiah 28:10 KJV.

70. Herbert Lockyer, *All the Men / All the Women* Compilation (Grand Rapids, MI: Zondervan, 2005).

71. As recognized by Oxford Dictionaries, this Word of the Year was from 2016. Although *Haverim* was originally published in 2013, edits to this section were made during its revision, which was re-released in 2017.

72. You can read the full article by Dave Magill at https://www.threadsuk.com/how-does-the-church-survive-a-post-truth-society, accessed November 17, 2016.

73. To learn more about master classes offered on study, discipleship, and more, visit master-classsuite.com.

74. As of this printing, the book *Shalom: How to Reach Anyone Anywhere* by Paul Clayton Gibbs is due to be published in 2018 by Harris House Publishing.

75. 1 Samuel 3:1-5.

76. 1 Samuel 3:8-10.

77. James 4:2.

78. William H. Gates III, *Business @ the Speed of Thought: Succeeding in the Digital Economy* (London: Penguin Group, 1999).

About the Author

Paul Clayton Gibbs is the founder and global director of Pais. He and his wife Lynn have two sons, Joel and Levi. Originally from Manchester, England, the Gibbs family moved to the USA in 2005 to globally expand Paul's vision of "missionaries making missionaries."

Paul began pioneering openings into Manchester schools as an associate minister in 1987. In September 1992, he founded the Pais Project, initially a one-team gap year project in north Manchester, which has exploded globally, training and placing thousands of missionaries and reaching millions of students throughout Europe, North and South America, Africa, Asia, and Australia. Since then, Paul has pioneered two other branches of Pais: one that equips churches in missional strategies and one that provides businesses with cause marketing strategies. Under Paul's leadership, the Pais Movement continues to grow, launching initiatives and resources to further God's Kingdom.

Paul gained national recognition in the UK for mentoring and training leaders. He has written several books and speaks throughout the world at venues, which include Bible colleges and seminaries, churches, leadership retreats, and youth conferences. His primary topics are pioneering, leadership development, the Kingdom of God, and ancient practices for postmodern times.

Paul enjoys swimming, surfing, skiing, sailing, snowboarding, and is an avid Manchester United fan!

paulgibbs.info
facebook.com/paulcgibbs
twitter.com/paulcgibbs

About the Pais Movement

Our Aim

Pais exists to spark a global movement, where the primary concern of God's people is His Kingdom, and where they are equipped to advance it in their world. We do this through distinctive approaches to mission, discipleship, and study in the areas of youth and schools, churches, and businesses.

Our Passion

Pais is the New Testament Greek word for 'child' or 'child servant to the king.' Our motto is 'missionaries making missionaries.' We are passionate about the people of our world and are desperate to see them in the relationship with God that He intended us to have. We come alongside schools, churches, and businesses in their endeavor to empower people to grow in their understanding and experience of God.

Our Vision

Mission lies at the heart of Pais. We seek to help both the apprentices and those they touch develop missionary hearts, missionary skills, and missionary lives. As each missionary makes a missionary, we see our world change.

paismovement.com
facebook.com/paismovement
twitter.com/paismovement

To learn more about the Pais Movement, watch the documentary.

'THE SPIRIT of a PIONEER'

a film about the four stages of vision

'Inspirational & Informative!'
Based on the book "The Line and the Dot" by Paul Clayton Gibbs

TheSpiritofaPioneerFilm.com
Free to view on **vimeo**

FREE CHRISTIAN
GAP YEAR!
INCLUDING FULL TRAINING, ACCOMMODATION AND MEALS

CHOOSE THE COMMUNITY YOU SERVE:

YOUTH

BUSINESSES

CHURCHES

ORGANIZATION

CHOOSE THE NATION YOU SERVE:

EUROPE
NORTH AMERICA
ASIA
AFRICA
SOUTH AMERICA
AUSTRALIA

www.paismovement.com

FREE GAP YEAR INCLUDES:
200 LECTURE HOURS | 1800 EXPERIENTIAL HOURS
BI-WEEKLY MENTORING | FULL APPRENTICESHIP

CHOOSE YOUR COURSE AND SPECIALIZATION:

YOUTH
SPORT
MUSIC
PERFORMING ARTS
PERSONALIZED
[DEVELOP YOUR GIFT]

ORGANIZATION
MEDIA
FINANCE
TRAINING
COMMUNICATION
HUMAN RESOURCES

CHURCHES
CHURCH PLANTING
COLLEGE MINISTRY
COMMUNITY OUTREACH

BUSINESSES
TEAM COACHING
SOCIAL RESPONSIBILITY
COMPANY MANAGEMENT

OPTIONAL UPGRADES
ACCREDITED CERTIFICATES AND DEGREES ARE AVAILABLE WITH A PAIS APPRENTICESHIP

apply | www.paismovement.com

Harris House Publishing

harrishousepublishing.com

Other Books from
Harris House Publishing

Available through harrishousepublishing.com and amazon.com.

By Karen Sebastian

The Power of Hope for Prodigals
Discover practical steps to establish hope in the midst of dark times. Learn how to see your child through the Father's eyes. Speak words of hope and encouragement. Prepare the way home—it's shorter than you think. Also available in Spanish.

The Power of Hope in Mourning
True grief is often messy, raw, and random, with waves of sadness washing over you. Hope Catalyst Karen Sebastian teaches you to 'ride' those waves, demonstrating how the very pain that threatens to destroy you can push you into the presence of God where hope and healing await.

By Katie Hopmann

The King's Invitation
Follow the travels of a boy on his journey to see the King. Meeting others along the way, he becomes loaded down with well-meaning gifts and advice. It's a lot to carry! Will he make it to the Royal City? Or will he give up?

By Mark Nathan Riley

Because You're Loved
Show the Faith. Share the Faith. Bring the Faith. This simple guide equips groups of believers with the tools to become a catalyst of transformation in their community.

By Paul Clayton Gibbs

The Ancient Trilogy

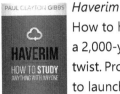

Haverim

How to help anyone study anything. This unique book takes a 2,000-year-old method of Bible study and gives it a modern twist. Providing step-by-step guidance, Paul Gibbs equips you to launch your own group study using Haverim Devotions.™

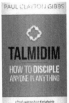

Talmidim

How to disciple anyone in anything. Helping us fundamentally rethink our current methods of discipleship, Paul Gibbs gives a fresh understanding of the Great Commission. By researching and applying Jesus's method of discipleship, Gibbs provides a simple template anyone can use.

Shalom

How to reach anyone anywhere. This book will show you how to embrace a fresh approach to missions. Coming 2017.

The Kingdom Trilogy

The Kingdom Pioneers

Do you have an idea, a vision, a passion to bring about change? In this completely revised second edition, Paul Gibbs equips you to navigate the four stages of vision and prepares you to pass the tests each stage brings. This book forewarns and forearms you, so you can see your vision fulfilled.

The Kingdom Principles

Debunking the perception that following Christ means following a list of rules, Paul Gibbs unpacks six Kingdom Principles that can transform your relationship with God from a life of rules to one of love.

The Kingdom Patterns

Have you ever lost track of God's direction for your life? Author Paul Gibbs provides practical guidance for discovering God's purpose in your life by showing you how to ask better questions of God in order to get better answers.

#haverimdevotions

JOIN THE DISCUSSION
haverimdevotions.com